Women *of* Influence

Women *of* Influence

Honorary Alumnae of Russell Sage College

of The Sage Colleges

KATHLEEN A. DONNELLY

Women *of*
Influence Honorary Alumnae of Russell Sage College of The Sage Colleges
Copyright © 2015 by Kathleen A. Donnelly

Printed in the United States of America

The Troy Book Makers • Troy, New York • thetroybookmakers.com

ISBN: 978-1-61468-318-6

Dedication

This work is dedicated to Dennis B. Tillman, who always supported my work, and was a steadfast advocate of the recognition of women's accomplishments.

Contents

Acknowledgements

I would like to thank Abigail Stambach, Archivist of The Sage Colleges. Abby cheerfully opened the Archives of The Sage Colleges to me and was a great resource as I searched for information about Honorary Degree recipients from Sage. She located documents and photographs and introduced me to the world of archives.

Nancy Ianucci, Archivist at the Emma Willard School, allowed me access to archives from the time in which Russell Sage College was a project of the Emma Willard Board of Trustees. Sarah Malcolm, Archivist at the FDR Presidential Library, searched for information about Eleanor Roosevelt and her Honorary Degrees. Melody Davis, faculty member of The Sage Colleges, gave me a quick tutorial on the life and work of Doris Emrick Lee. I also talked to archivists at the University of Wisconsin, Purdue University, Columbia University, New York University, and Bates College to verify dates.

Carol Furman, Bonnie Hagan, Carol Kapsner, Abby Stambach, Sara Schuman, and Sharon Robinson read drafts, corrected grammar, and made suggestions. I am grateful for their support.

Lisa Brainard, Director of Libraries and the Troy Library Faculty and Staff, especially Stacey Civello, Joyce Cockerham, Nicole Johnson, Dan Palmer, Amy Pass, Dianne Roosa, Regina Vertone, Terry Wasielewski, and Chris White were both welcoming and very helpful as I ventured into an endeavor that was different from anything I had done before.

Joan Clifford, Director of Alumnae Relations and Executive Director of the Russell Sage College Alumnae Association, graciously allowed me to use the RSC Alumnae Archives. Tiffany Mangino Gyrus, and Nicolle Otty pointed me in the right direction within the archives.

I would also like to thank Susan Scrimshaw, President of The Sage Colleges, and Rose Grignon, Executive Assistant to the President, for their support.

Any errors or misinterpretations are my responsibility.

Preface

Several years ago, I had a casual conversation with a colleague who confessed to knowing little about the recipients of Honorary Degrees from The Sage Colleges. This prompted me to find the specific achievements for which Russell Sage College and later The Sage Colleges had selected Honorary Degree recipients. Although the recipients were accomplished in many different fields and in times of different expectations and sensibilities, some common themes emerged from their stories.

Many of the women whose stories I selected encountered overt as well as covert discrimination that was based significantly on gender. In some cases, they also experienced discrimination based on race and/or ethnicity. They faced this discrimination head on, often in different ways. Some resigned coveted positions in protest while others sidestepped the discrimination by transferring their efforts to a corollary field that did not yet have a strong male presence. Some, who were economically able, volunteered in a chosen field when they were unable to find a paying job. Eventually, whatever the path they took, they performed at a very high level at which point they could no longer be relegated to the background.

As many of these women pursued their careers, their contributions were downplayed, ignored or even usurped in favor of male colleagues. This phenomenon was coined the *Matilda Effect* by Margaret W. Rossiter.[1] Recognition of these women with Honorary Degrees and continued public acknowledgement of their accomplishments can counterbalance the Matilda Effect.

Whatever their fields, whatever their choices, these women had determination and self-confidence in their abilities. They recognized what was important to them and worked toward their goals, going over, under and/or around obstacles. Some came from wealth and privilege, some from the other end of the socioeconomic spectrum, and some from the middle. This work was not an attempt to write a comprehensive biography of these individuals. Instead it is a snapshot of their lives with an extensive list of resources for those who wish to learn more.

---

[1] Margaret W. Rossiter, "The Matilda Effect in Science," *Social Studies of Science* 23 (1993): 325-41.

This is only a sampling of women who have been honored by Russell Sage College and The Sage Colleges. It is, I think, a representative group of Honorary Alumnae.

All deserve to be remembered and honored as Women of Influence.

James L. Meader, Ph.D.

Second President of Russell Sage College

James Laurence Meader (1893-1974) was the second President of Russell Sage College (RSC). Initially appointed in 1928, he served for 14 years. It was a time of great change, within RSC and in the wider community, and Meader would play a major role in both communities.

At the time of his appointment he was one of the youngest private college Presidents in the country. It is worthwhile to see the person he was, so as to better understand the foundation he established for RSC. James Meader was a New Englander with roots in Maine and New Hampshire. He was a 1915 graduate of Bates College. He subsequently earned an A.M. (Psychology and Education, 1923) and Ph.D. (Psychology, Philosophy, and College Administration, 1928) from Columbia University. His early career was in Connecticut with increasing responsibilities in higher education.

His formal education and his work experiences marked Meader as a visionary and innovator in higher education, a man who would try new things while building on what was already in place. Russell Sage College, established in 1916, was the ideal setting for Meader to implement his vision. He was keenly interested in the intersection of educational institutions and the larger community and how that interaction could enhance students' education. While President of RSC, he put into practice what he espoused, serving at various times as President of the Troy Chamber of Commerce, the Troy Public Library, the Troy Council of Social Agencies, and as a member of Samaritan Hospital's Board of Trustees.

In one of the first acts of his presidency, Meader established an Honorary Degree program to recognize individuals who had made significant contributions to their communities and had the potential for continuing to make contributions. He established the procedures by which candidates were chosen, often seeking out women of influence. During his presidency, over fifty honorary degrees were awarded, greater than ninety percent to women.

The first Honorary Degrees were awarded in Meader's second year as President. The inaugural degrees went to Eliza Kellas, the founding President of Russell

Sage College, and Anna Eleanor Roosevelt, First Lady of New York State and eventually First Lady of the United States, a diplomat and force for change.

Initially, Dr. Meader led the way in nominating and bestowing Honorary Degrees on behalf of the College, but as was his pattern, he got others involved. A committee was established with membership from the faculty, administration and the Board of Trustees. Honorary Degree recipients were encouraged to remain involved with the college and often served as members of the honorary degree selection committee and/or were appointed to the Board of Trustees. As noted by President McKinstry in 1946, Dr. Meader's method for determining candidates was continued, including the practice of seeking outstanding women candidates.

Dr. Meader guided the growth of RSC during a time of much economic upheaval. On September 9, 1929, within months of his inauguration and a short time before the Stock Market Crash of 1929, he signed an agreement to merge the New York City Central School of Hygiene and Physical Education, headed by Helen McKinstry, with RSC. After a year, the new program and its faculty physically moved to Troy. Unfortunately, the economic conditions of the era prevented the planned expansion of the Physical Education Program and movement of the merged Central School and RSC to land owned by RSC on the outskirts of Troy. Nevertheless, the two distinct cultures successfully meshed and flourished under Meader's leadership, with McKinstry's enthusiastic cooperation.

Meader became interested in the Little Theater Movement, perhaps through his talks with Eve Le Gallienne, an actress active in civic and community theater, who was awarded an Honorary Degree by RSC in 1930. John Campbell, the head of the RSC Maintenance Department, built a Little Theater on the foundations of the former garages for the student residences, the Kellas and Boardman Houses. The first production was the experimental play *Cradle Song*, a favorite of Le Gallienne.

In 1935 he introduced a four-year nursing degree at RSC. Once again, this endeavor required careful interaction with other groups to achieve a goal that was strengthened by the synergy. In this case, the other entities were the Albany Hospital and the Albany Medical College. The new program was modeled after one established at Yale by Annie Warburton Goodrich and used the recommendations of the National Committee on the Grading of Nursing Schools. Goodrich was awarded an Honorary Degree from RSC in 1936.

Students were encouraged to become aware of global opportunities. In 1936 a French House was opened. In 1939 Meader established a Spanish House as an additional way for students to become proficient in Spanish. He foresaw "increasing opportunities for college-trained women in countries where Spanish is spoken."[2]

Dr. Meader laid out his vision for the college and the students in lengthy addresses to the college community and in his reports to the Board of Trustees. Although not all of these addresses and reports have been preserved, we can get a sense of Dr. Meader's charisma and leadership from those that remain. In 1938 he "delineated criteria for the admissibility of new students to the field of higher learning. These, he believes, should transcend matters of scholarship or academic standing. They include a way of thinking and living."[3]

Meader also challenged the faculty by instituting changes in the administrative culture of RSC. He established a committee-based governance system. He noted, "the time had passed when decisions on educational policy could efficiently be left in the hands of an individual."[4] Faculty-elected participants had a decisive voice in formulating and deciding educational policies.

His addresses to the college community were often designed to foster discussion of important global issues. In 1934 he addressed global tensions with a speech excerpted on the Opinion page of the *New York Times*.

"I renounce war for what it does to our men. I renounce war for what it forces us to do to other human beings who for the time being we call our

---

[2] "Russell Sage Gets a Spanish House," *New York Times,* October 15, 1939, *ProQuest Historical Newspapers: The New York Times (1851-2010) with Index (1851-1933)* (103089431).

[3] "Tells Who Belongs At Russell Sage: Dr. Meader Puts Thinking and Living Before Scholarship in College Education," *New York Times,* November 6, 1938, *ProQuest Historical Newspapers: The New York Times (1851-2010) with Index (1851-1933)* (102411057).

[4] "Russell Sage Widens Faculty Influence: Council to Have Decisive Voice in Educational Policies," *New York Times* December 11, 1938 *ProQuest Historical Newspapers: The New York Times (1851-2010) with Index (1851-1933)* (102492326).

enemies. I renounce war for its consequences, for the lives it lives on and for the financial, social, economic and moral ruin which follow in its train."

"Finally, I renounce war for its futility. This last war settled no arguments for any length of time. The French still fear the Germans. The Germans still hate the French—with an even greater hatred than before. For these reasons do I renounce war and I solemnly swear that never again will I sanction another war."[5]

At the opening convocation of 1939, Meader called for the immediate repeal of the Neutrality Act. The Neutrality Act prohibited the export of "arms, ammunition, and implements of war" from the United States to foreign nations at war and required arms manufacturers in the United States to apply for an export license. His argument was that if aid were not supplied to England and France, then the United States would eventually have to fight Hitler unaided. However, he urged the students to make up their own minds. He invited faculty and staff who disagreed with him to make their arguments to the students at subsequent addresses.

Ten months before the Japanese attack on Pearl Harbor, Meader announced that he had increasingly involved the Russell Sage Community in preparing "to defend our land from invasion by the armed forces of a foreign nation and our form of government from the invasion of foreign ideologies."[6] He linked national defense to the preservation and strengthening of institutions of higher education, such as Russell Sage College.

Further, Meader explained why he thought the program was necessary within a college environment. "We must not emphasize the necessity of guns, ammunition, tanks, planes and ships to the neglect of those institutions that minister to the happiness, physical well-being, mental development of our one hundred and thirty million citizens. What will it profit us to become the strongest nation in the world in terms of the munitions and impliments [sic] of war if we allow the well-springs of education, health, civic competence and spiritual enlightenment to dry up? . . . With every great European nation

---

[5] James L. Meader, "Futility of War," *New York Times* November 11, 1934 *ProQuest Historical Newspapers: The New York Times (1851-2010) with Index (1851-1933)* (101202102).

[6] Meader Report to the Board of Trustees, February 5, 1941, Archives and Special Collections, The Sage Colleges, Troy, NY.

submerged by war, the United States remains the only great power whose people are still in a position to maintain the institutions of public enlightenment and service which are civilization's center and source of progress."[7]

He instituted a Defense Program involving students and faculty that had three components: Building Morale; Offering Emergency Skill Courses; and British Relief. This program, a mix of academic discussion of aspects of democracy, practical course work, and fund raising, generated interest from other organizations attempting to involve their communities in defense work.

Meader strengthened the college through its course offerings and hiring of credentialed faculty, and through seeking and receiving full accreditation by the Association of American Universities (AAU) and the American Association of University Women (AAUW). On December 7, 1941, the Imperial Japanese Navy attacked Pearl Harbor. With the accreditations in hand and the United States at war, Dr. Meader asked for a leave of absence so that he could take an active role in the defense of the country. Dr. Meader said, "With the college fully accredited and with the strongest faculty we have ever had, I believe that others can carry on and that my first duty now is to the Nation."[8]

The leave was granted effective March 31, 1942, and Dr. Meader was sworn into the U.S. Army as a Major, initially assigned to Office of the Chief of Ordnance, Washington. A year later, he formally resigned as President of Russell Sage. He continued to serve in the Army for the duration of the war and the immediate aftermath, both in the states and abroad, primarily in Southeastern Asia. He was with General MacArthur at the liberation of the Philippines and one of his postwar responsibilities was to reestablish municipal government in Dagupan, Philippines. He later served with the Department of State as First Secretary, Public Affairs Officer at Manila, Malaya, and Thailand.

Dr. Meader never returned to Russell Sage College in a professional capacity and there is no evidence that he visited the college or Troy after the war. His war and postwar experiences led to a position as Director of Community Affairs at the East-West Center at the University of Hawaii and as founding

---

[7] Ibid.

[8] Undated letter from James L. Meader to the Board of Trustees requesting a year long leave of absence, Archives and Special Collections, The Sage Colleges, Troy, NY.

President of Hawai'i Pacific University, Honolulu, Hawai'i. Dr. Meader died on October 31, 1974 in Honolulu.

In 1979 the Little Theater begun by Meader in 1932, reopened after being closed for renovations made possible by gifts from Elizabeth Perkins Green '28 and the Fiftieth Reunion Class of 1929. At the opening ceremony, the building was named the James L. Meader Little Theater.

When Meader established the system for selecting individuals to receive an Honorary Degree from Russell Sage College, he emphasized recognition of individuals who had made significant contributions to their communities and had the potential to continue their contributions. Using these criteria, Meader would have been a candidate for an Honorary Degree from RSC. However, he never publically received one.

Each year that Dr. Meader served as President of Russell Sage College, he was involved in the selection of recipients who had an impact that led to the greater good. The following pages include a representative sampling of individuals who were honored as Honorary Degree recipients of Russell Sage College or The Sage Colleges.

Eliza Kellas, B.A.

DOCTOR OF LAWS-1929

First President of Russell Sage College, Head of Emma Willard School, Educator

Eliza Kellas (1864-1943) was born on a farm in Franklin County, New York, to a naturalized Scottish immigrant father and a mother from an influential Canadian family. Her formal education began in a one-room district school. At sixteen, due to a sudden opening in that school, Kellas began teaching there.

Kellas attended the Potsdam Normal School (now the State University of New York at Potsdam) from 1887-89, and earned a diploma in 1889. The following year, she was listed as a faculty member of the school. While Kellas was a student and faculty member at Potsdam Normal School, the school underwent a transition from a liberal arts based academy to a school for training teachers. She came away from her time at Potsdam with an appreciation of both traditions.

In September 1891 she was appointed Principal of the School of Practice at Plattsburgh Normal School (now the State University of New York at Plattsburgh). By 1895 Kellas had assumed the role of Preceptress, analogous to that of a present day Dean of Students. During her time in Plattsburgh, she used summer vacations to travel and take courses at other institutions. In 1901 Kellas resigned her Plattsburgh position to assume the role of governess to the three small children of her recently widowed friend and women's education pioneer, Mary Lyon Cheney.

After Cheney's remarriage in 1905, the family, including Eliza Kellas, settled in Cambridge, Massachusetts. Kellas took advantage of being in Cambridge to enroll at Radcliffe, although at forty, she was older than most of the other students. She earned her bachelor's degree in 1910 and after a summer trip exploring Iceland, she returned to Radcliffe to enroll in graduate school. Kellas did not finish the year, however, because she accepted the position of Headmistress of the Emma Willard School (EWS) in February 1911.

Through the generosity of Mrs. Russell Sage (Margaret Olivia Slocum Sage) in 1910, EWS relocated from downtown Troy to the site of the present EWS, which was then on the outskirts of Troy. Enrollment had declined and standards had eroded in the years before the move and Kellas was charged with increasing enrollments and raising standards.

By late winter of 1915, Mrs. Sage was sufficiently impressed by Kellas' work that Mrs. Sage summoned her to New York City to offer her a proposition. Mrs. Sage was interested in using the buildings in downtown Troy vacated by EWS for a college for women. This college would offer young women a practical education grounded in the liberal arts, but Mrs. Sage would only agree to provide the funds if Kellas would assume leadership of the college. Since Kellas would retain the Headmistress position of EWS as well, she agonized over her decision. Within a day or two, Kellas accepted the challenge, aware that if she declined, there would be no funds available for founding a college for women in Troy. The new institution was to open in September 1916.

Establishing a new college would have been a major challenge even without the short time frame and the fact that the designated President had another full-time position. The future Russell Sage College (RSC) had to meet rigorous requirements for faculty, equipment, curriculum, and degrees set by the chartering entity, the Board of Regents of the State of New York. Without a charter, an institution cannot legally operate as a degree-granting institution. Chartering was complicated because the terms of Mrs. Sage's donation gave the money to the Board of Trustees of EWS, who in her view would found the college as a project of EWS.

In September 1917 the Board of Regents of New York State approved an amendment to the EWS charter, changing its corporate name to Emma Willard School and Russell Sage College. That meant that for its first year of operation RSC operated without a charter. For the following ten years (1917-1927), RSC did not have an independent charter and could not grant degrees in its own name. Once RSC was independent, a Board of Trustees separate from that of EWS was appointed.

The amendment to the EWS charter required the approval of the Board of Regents of New York State and the EWS Board of Trustees. A major issue was the manner in which Mrs. Sage had donated the money for RSC through the EWS Board of Trustees. The Board of Regents of New York State was concerned about the lack of clarity surrounding the endowment for RSC. While attending to her duties as President of RSC and Headmistress of EWS, Kellas skillfully and diplomatically facilitated a resolution to these issues. It was an exhausting task carried out through letters, personal meetings and travel to New York City where the increasingly infirm Mrs. Sage was residing.

Once RSC was independent from EWS, Kellas divided the money Mrs. Sage had given to EWS to establish RSC. Kellas did this in accordance with what she assumed to be Mrs. Sage's wishes from conversations prior to Sage's death in 1918.

In the nine months between Eliza Kellas' acceptance of Mrs. Sage's proposal to start a college and the opening, there were enormous tasks to be completed. In addition to chartering the institution, Sage Hall, Gurley Hall, and the Plum Building had to be renovated. They had been vacant for five years and needed extensive work. Faculty and staff had to be hired, curricula devised, and students recruited. Kellas said that she would have been happy with twenty-five students that first year. When the doors opened, there were 117 students from at least six states, Puerto Rico, and Hawaii. For the first twelve years of the existence of RSC, Eliza Kellas dealt with the administrative issues of RSC, acquired and renovated buildings, met with Trustees, faculty, and attorneys while she interacted with the Board of Regents of New York State. Kellas tried to steer a course through the legal and financial difficulties imposed by the founding of RSC as a project of the EWS Board of Trustees, while still retaining the Headmistress position at EWS. She divided her time, mornings at RSC, completing RSC business, and the remaining time at EWS, doing EWS business. It was an enormous task.

During this time period her sister—Katherine Kellas—became the first Dean of the college. Although Katherine Kellas lived at Emma Willard, her full time position was at RSC, where she was in charge of daily academic life. The Kellas and Kellas team proved to be extremely successful.

On December 29, 1927 the Board of Regents of New York State granted a new and separate charter for Russell Sage College, and the Emma Willard School was reaffirmed as a secondary school only. Anticipating the action of the Board of Regents, the Kellas sisters submitted their resignations to the RSC Board in 1926, planning to return to full time status at EWS. The RSC Board requested that they wait until a successor had been found. On February 6, 1928 their resignations were finally accepted.

In her twenty-three page address at the inauguration of her successor on February 24, 1928, Kellas stated her hope that RSC and EWS would have been merged so "that in time it would become an educational shrine. That plan was not deemed feasible, and we are to proceed along different lines."[9]

She praised President Meader as an "educator, young, vigorous, progressive and wise . . . who would now lead a young institution started by . . . men and women who gave their best to this infant institution, when most things were hoped for and but few seen. Their faith, loyalty and courage made it possible to turn over to you a fairly sturdy youngster."[10]

In his first year President Meader initiated the granting of Honorary Degrees. Eliza Kellas and Anna Eleanor Roosevelt comprised the inaugural class. Eliza Kellas became the first RSC recipient of the degree of Doctor of Laws and Anna Eleanor Roosevelt the first RSC recipient of the degree of Doctor of Humane Letters.

On June 13, 1929 the degree of Doctor of Laws was conferred on Eliza Kellas by Russell Sage College, recognizing her as an "outstanding educational executive and administrator. . . . It was your foresight and far-reaching vision that brought this institution into existence…Russell Sage College is the child of your head, your heart and your hands, and this child rises up today to call you blessed, and to confer upon you its highest honor."[11]

After her resignation as President of RSC, Kellas resumed her full-time position at Emma Willard. She continued in that role until her retirement in 1942 when she moved to an apartment in Troy. After being weakened by a case of influenza, she died on April 10, 1943.

---

[9] Eliza Kellas, Address given on February 24, 1928, Archives and Special Collections, Emma Willard School, Troy, NY.

[10] Ibid.

[11] Honorary Degree Collection, Archives and Special Collections, The Sage Colleges, Troy, NY.

Anna Eleanor Roosevelt

DOCTOR OF HUMANE LETTERS-1929

First Lady of New York State, First Lady of U.S.A., Delegate to the UN, RSC Trustee

Anna Eleanor Roosevelt (1884-1962) was born into a prominent New York family descended from Claes Martenszen van Rosenvelt, an emigrant from Holland to New Amsterdam around 1649. She was named after her mother, Anna Hall, but was called Eleanor (ER). Orphaned by the age of nine, Eleanor and her siblings moved into their maternal grandmother's home in Tivoli, New York. They continued to have frequent contact with their father's brother, Theodore (TR) and his family. TR took a special interest in Eleanor. TR would eventually become the 26th President of the United States.

ER was a keen observer of contemporary life. Her travels abroad and her close connections with TR expanded her outlook beyond her narrow social world. She attended a convent school in Italy and a boarding school in England, but she always regretted not attending college.

While in England, she began to develop a social conscience that championed the rights of the working class and became aware of others as people with needs and wants. She had looked up to her uncle TR and was influenced by his idealism. TR also taught her the power of organized political reform and the crucial process necessary to establish fair labor practices.

As a debutante, ER was expected to participate in charity work that would improve the lives of less fortunate New Yorkers. During her debutante year, ER began to work to better the lives of impoverished women, including teaching dance and calisthenics at the Rivington Settlement House. The classes showed immigrants how to use physical movement to improve their health, especially after long hours of tedious work in confined spaces. From 1903-05 she was an investigator for The Consumer's League in New York City. She visited workers in their tenements and workplaces and documented their living and working conditions as well as labor practices.

Manufacturers who produced products under certain labor conditions such as paid overtime and who hired workers a minimum of 16 years old were given the "Consumer's White Label." ER began to use the media via pamphlets, press releases, and letters to the editor to inform and disseminate information about The Consumer's League endorsement of these White Label manufacturers.

In 1905 ER married Franklin Delano Roosevelt (FDR) in New York City. President Theodore Roosevelt walked his niece down the aisle and stole the spotlight. There are no pictures of the newly married couple on their wedding day but there are, however, many pictures of TR.

FDR and ER had a common ancestor, Claes Martenszen van Rosenvelt, and were fifth cousins once removed. ER's father, Elliot, TR's brother, was FDR's godfather. With their marriage, the Republican Oyster Bay, Long Island and the Democratic Hudson Valley Roosevelt families were joined.

FDR followed his distant cousin TR's career intently; he admired, and in many ways modeled his early life after TR's. Until he met Eleanor, FDR had little direct knowledge of the underprivileged and working classes and although he supported TR's reforms, he had little exposure to the realities of their daily lives. ER brought him to tenement houses to show him how immigrants in New York City lived and to factories to see their working conditions first-hand. One of ER's greatest accomplishments was to bring the lives of the lower classes into FDR's consciousness.

As FDR began his political career, ER continued to expand his worldview and advocate for those who were less fortunate. She had six children, one of whom died in infancy. She fulfilled the social obligations required of each of FDR's offices. She continued her volunteer work in many organizations, including The Women's City Club of New York, The Women's Trade Union League, The League of Women Voters, The World Peace Movement, and the Bok Peace Prize Committee. In 1926, she co-founded and ran Val-Kill Industries, a factory that employed jobless Hyde Park craftsman to build furniture. She started, co-owned, and taught at the Todhunter School for Girls on the East Side of New York City. She became a writer, lecturer, and a radio show commentator. On January 1, 1929, she added the title of First Lady of New York State to her long list of obligations and interests.

It was also during that year that Russell Sage College awarded Honorary Degrees for the first time; the degree of Doctor of Laws to the founding President of RSC, Eliza Kellas, and the degree of Doctor of Humane Letters to Anna Eleanor Roosevelt. The citation for ER's degree is particularly noteworthy because it connects the selection of ER as an Honorary Degree recipient with the ideals of the young college. This was the first of thirty-five Honorary Degrees awarded to ER.

On June 13, 1929 the degree of Doctor of Humane Letters was conferred on Anna Eleanor Roosevelt by Russell Sage College, in recognition of her multiple contributions as "teacher, educational administrator, director of industry; guiding spirit of many civic and legislative organizations, active associate in many public and private philanthropic movements; First Lady of the Empire State, Russell Sage College considers you one of the ablest, most energetic and most versatile women in public life today. One of the purposes of this College is to send out into the world women who have the desire and the ability to produce something which society needs, to carry on some constructive, upbuilding [sic] activity, to participate creatively in the work of the world. Our College aims not at leisure but leadership, and stresses the importance of dedicating one's self to service in the interests of one's home, one's community, one's state and one's nation. We have chosen to honor you today because we feel that you exemplify with distinction those ideals for which our College stands."[12]

ER's accomplishments after she received the Honorary Degree from RSC were extensive and profound. Discussion of even a small selection of them would exceed the limited space available for this entry. ER always became engaged in the communities in which she lived and worked. The increasingly public role she assumed as First Lady of New York and then First Lady of the United States required that she give up, at least publically, her role in activities that might present an apparent or real conflict of interest. As well, she had to avoid endeavors that were too obviously partisan. Within those constraints, she made continued contributions to a wide variety of enterprises.

As First Lady of New York, she was a significant force behind the promotion of Frances Perkins to head of the State Industrial Relations Commission and of Perkins's appointment as Commissioner of the New York State Department of Labor. Perkins would be appointed by FDR in 1933 as the United States Secretary of Labor, the first woman to be appointed to a cabinet position. ER was involved in FDR's reform of the Public Employment Service and became FDR's eyes and ears as an unofficial inspector of state-supported

---

[12] Ibid.

institutions that served vulnerable populations, such as orphans, the elderly, children, and the sick. She learned to do her own inspections, checking garages, kitchens, plumbing, and electricity, rather than accepting the "official" word of those in charge.

When ER became the First Lady of the United States on March 4, 1933, her platform became larger and more public. She had to be more circumspect as her words and actions had greater impact. As First Lady she continued her work as an advocate for women's issues, the underprivileged, and education. She was in the public eye more than earlier First Ladies and continued her work as a writer, public speaker, and media figure. This gave her an unparalled opportunity to inform the public and to promote discussion about issues she considered important, but it also made her a controversial figure and a target for attack. Her public activist role forever changed the potential role of a First Lady.

During the Great Depression, as employment became scarce, women often lost their positions disproportionately to men in comparable jobs Many positions were also closed to women and women journalists were an especially vulnerable group. Presidential press conferences were restricted to male journalists, while the women journalists covered issues like fashion and décor. Two days after the 1933 inauguration, ER held the first of her 348 press conferences as First Lady. Twenty-four journalists, all women, attended; no men were allowed. Forty news organizations were granted credentials to participate in ER's press conferences, but the journalists had to be women. Thus, large and small news organizations had to employ women journalists if they wanted access to the conferences coordinated through the President's office. Sometimes a political decision was made to release information through ER's press conferences rather than directly from the President's Office or the West Wing. This action served to elevate women reporters as professionals and it also led to women journalists becoming a permanent part of the modern White House Press Corps. ER's actions gave the women journalists a platform where they could showcase their credibility as reporters of substantive news.

The pressures of the twin crises of his administration—the Great Depression and WWII—coupled with his physical limitations due to polio, prevented FDR from traveling around the country to interact with constituents and to see firsthand whether New Deal programs were having the impact he envisioned. ER became ever more important as FDR's eyes and ears. She traveled alone, without secret service protection, and often unannounced. These visits allowed her to get a realistic view of the implementation of programs. Analogous to her influence as the First Lady of New York, ER's input from inspections was crucial to the fine-tuning and success of many of these federal programs.

Sometimes ER was far ahead of her husband, both politically and socially. A case in point was racial equality. She believed more strongly than FDR and many in the government that the federal government had a moral duty to lead the way in ensuring racial equality. This was a radical concept for many and almost treasonous to others. She showed her support for racial equality through word and deed. She was photographed at a 1938 conference in Birmingham, Alabama sitting in the middle of an aisle between the "whites-only" and "colored-only" sections. Most famously, she publically resigned from the Daughters of the American Revolution after they refused to rent their facility, Constitution Hall, for a concert by the acclaimed contralto, Marian Anderson, because she was African-American. Two months later, ER invited Anderson to sing in the White House for the King and Queen of England. The lengthy list of ER's achievements continued throughout the more than twelve years of FDR's time in office. Eight months after FDR's death, President Harry Truman appointed ER to the first American delegation to the United Nations on December 31, 1945.

As an honorary alumna, ER continued her association with RSC for many years. She nominated candidates for Honorary Degrees and served on the Board of Trustees. She resigned from the board on April 29, 1946, because her obligations as a member of the American delegation to the United Nations left her unable to devote sufficient time to RSC.

In the United Nations, ER had an international platform. When the United Nations established a permanent Commission on Human Rights, ER was unanimously elected chair. She chaired the subcommittee charged with writing the Universal Declaration of Human Rights (UDHR) and her skillful, diplomatic, and persistent leadership of a group from many cultures, ethnicities, and political systems led to the formulation of a document that passed the committee unanimously. When she presented the UDHR to the General Assembly for adoption on December 10, 1948, she received an unprecedented standing ovation. Such an action has not been repeated for a single delegate. Since the United Nations had no enforcement powers for the

UDHR, ER traveled the globe investigating conditions and urging support for Human Rights and for the United Nations. She served as part of the American Delegation to the United Nations until December 31, 1952 when newly elected President Eisenhower asked for her resignation.

ER remained active in public life, even serving on the board of the Peace Corps during President Kennedy's administration, until shortly before her death. As her health deteriorated, she realized that she would be unable to continue an active role in areas that interested her and those close to her said that she was ready to die. To ER, inactivity was not something she could accept. Through her lifelong commitment to equal rights for all, Eleanor Roosevelt was an exemplary embodiment of the ideals of RSC cited by President Meader when he conferred RSC's Honorary Degree on her in 1929. She died on November 7, 1962 and is buried at Hyde Park next to FDR.

Lillian Moller Gilbreth, Ph.D., D.E.

DOCTOR OF SCIENCE-1931

Engineer, Pioneer in Industrial Organizational Management, Author, RSC Trustee

Lillian Moller Gilbreth (1878-1972) was born at a time when women's roles were narrowly defined. The oldest daughter of nine children, Gilbreth was tutored at home in her early years. She was regularly responsible for the care of her siblings, as her mother was often ill. Her parents were surprised that she wanted to attend college, as they thought a more fitting role would be to marry someone in her social class and assume the management of a household.

Gilbreth persisted with her desire to attend college and her parents allowed her to attend the University of California at Berkeley as long as she commuted from home and continued to take care of her siblings. Although Gilbreth encountered barriers due to her gender, she eventually earned advanced degrees in Literature (M.L., University of California), Engineering (M.E., University of Michigan), Psychology (Ph.D., Brown University), and Engineering (D.E., Rutgers University).

Married in 1904, Frank and Lillian Gilbreth were full partners and collaborators in Frank's construction business until it was sold. In 1912 they founded a management consulting business, Gilbreth, Inc.; they focused on time and motion, and fatigue studies for industry. After identifying eighteen standardized motions used in performing tasks, they labeled each as a *therblig* (gilbreth reversed after transposing the th). Workers performing a task would be filmed and the therbligs identified and analyzed. Unnecessary therbligs could be eliminated, increasing efficiency and reducing worker fatigue. Lillian was an equal partner in the highly successful business. She was married to Frank for twenty years, until he died suddenly of a heart attack in 1924. She gave birth to thirteen children; eleven survived to adulthood.

After her husband's death, however, Gilbreth found that the men in management positions were reluctant to hire her despite her earlier successes. So, she switched her focus to areas that at the time were the purview of women, domestic management and home economics. She developed an efficient model for a modern kitchen that she labeled as circular routing. This model, now known as the work triangle, is still used.

If she thought of something that would increase efficiency and reduce worker fatigue but wasn't available, she invented it. Often these inventions made some aspect of a woman's labor easier, such as refrigerator door shelves, a refrigerator butter keeper, an electric mixer, a trash can with a lid that could be opened by a foot pedal, a waste water hose system for a washing machine, even a *Gilbreth Management Desk* from which the housekeeper could efficiently run the house in a way that integrated the outside world and the life of the mind into homemaking. Increased efficiencies would make housekeeping only a part of a woman's life, not her whole existence. With more efficient ways of doing household tasks, the resultant savings in time and energy could be used in other ways, including paid employment outside the home unrelated to household work.

Gilbreth was a pioneer in what would come to be known as the field of industrial organizational management. Because of her diverse academic background, she was the first person to integrate psychology and industrial management in a consistent, scientific way. In addition, she used her engineering background and skills to invent tools that made tasks more efficient. Frank and Lillian Gilbreth organized their personal life using the principles they developed for industrial clients. After Frank's death, Lillian continued to use her home life as a laboratory.

On June 8, 1931 the degree of Doctor of Science was conferred on Dr. Gilbreth by Russell Sage College, recognizing her outstanding academic credentials and achievements, her industrial and government work, her body of written work and her success in her private life. Gilbreth continued to be actively involved in the life of RSC for many years, as a member of the Board of Trustees from 1944-46 and an Honorary Trustee from 1946-57. She was also involved in the selection of Honorary Degree recipients.

Gilbreth had a sixty-five year career in industrial engineering and management, always with a focus on the human element. She remained active professionally until she was ninety years old. During her long career, she received more than twenty Honorary Degrees. She was the second female member in the American Society of Mechanical Engineers and received the Henry Laurence

Gantt Medal for contributions to industrial engineering jointly with her late husband. Gilbreth was the first member of the Society of Women Engineers as well as the first woman elected to the National Academy of Engineering. For her contributions to motion studies, the intertwining of management, engineering and human relations and her efforts in modifying industrial and home environments so that the handicapped could be fully employed, she was awarded the Hoover Medal. She died on January 2, 1972 in Arizona.

Ruth Bryan Owen

DOCTOR OF HUMANE LETTERS-1931

First Elected Congresswoman from the South, First U.S. Woman Diplomat

Ruth Bryan (1885-1954) was born in Jacksonville, Illinois. The daughter of two lawyers, she was raised and educated in Lincoln, Nebraska and Washington, D.C. Her father, William Jennings Bryan, was active politically, first as the two-term United States Representative to Congress from Nebraska and then as a Presidential candidate. In her teen years, Bryan became a public figure in her own right as a social leader and was known for her charitable work.

Bryan attended the University of Nebraska at Lincoln, but she dropped out after two years to marry William H. Leavitt, an artist twice her age who was painting her father's portrait when they met. In her wedding announcement in the *New York Times*, September 9, 1903, her career was identified as that of a "belle." Bryan did travel as her father's secretary during his third presidential candidacy in 1908. Ruth and William Leavitt had two children, Ruth and John, before their marriage ended in divorce in 1909. ·

The next year Bryan married Lieutenant Reginald A. Owen of the Royal Engineer Corps of the British Army and together they had two children, Reginald and Helen. From the time of this marriage forward she was known as Ruth Bryan Owen (RBO). RBO accompanied her husband to his overseas posts, including extended time in Jamaica, then part of the British West Indies. During WWI, RBO served as secretary-treasurer of the American Women's War Relief Fund in London while her husband was on active duty. In 1915 RBO joined the British Volunteer Aid Detachment and served as a nurse to convalescent soldiers in Cairo. She also organized a group of volunteers, the *Optimists*, who entertained the wounded at military hospitals in the Middle East.

RBO's husband contracted trench nephritis during WWI and never recovered his full health. In 1919 the family moved to Florida to be near family and RBO began lecturing on the professional circuit to support her family. She was so successful that the University of Miami offered her a faculty position to teach the art of public speaking, which she did from 1926-28. After Major

Owen died in 1927, RBO decided to run for Congress with the support of her University of Miami students.

RBO won the election and was the first woman to be elected to Congress from the Deep South. Her defeated opponent, William C. Lawson, challenged her election, however, saying that she was not a U.S. citizen for the required seven years. Prior to the passage of The Cable Act of 1922, an American woman lost her American citizenship if she married a citizen of a foreign country; the husband's citizenship determined the wife's citizenship. Three years after The Cable Act passed, RBO moved to the U.S. and applied for restoration of her citizenship and her request was granted. Therefore, Governor Martin of Florida issued a certificate of election in November 1928 to RBO and she was sworn in as a member of Congress on April 15, 1929. Lawson then appealed to the Elections Committee of the House of Representatives and RBO's testimony was published in *The New York Times.* "No man was ever called before such a committee as this to explain his marriage. If there is any penalty for my marriage I bear it proudly. I ask this committee for nothing more than justice and I expect nothing less."[13] Her election stood.

On June 8, 1931 the degree of Doctor of Humane Letters was conferred on Ruth Bryan Owen by Russell Sage College, in recognition of her multiple talents as a lecturer, author and teacher. "We feel that few women in America today are doing more than you are to promote good citizenship, high ideals of home life, and sound training of children. Your keen feeling of responsibility for the betterment of home and school and state, and your efforts so to reorganize existing governmental agencies that these three great institutions may work side by side for the ultimate betterment of State and Nation, commands our highest respect and our heartiest approval."[14]

RBO was reelected to a second term in 1930. Among her notable achievements in Congress was the sponsorship and strong advocacy for the designation of the Florida Everglades as a National Park. She was also involved in passage

---

[13] "Mrs. Owens Defends Her Citizenship," *New York Times,* January 19, 1930, *ProQuest Historical Newspapers: The New York Times (1851-2010) with Index (1851-1933)* (99024915).

[14] Honorary Degree Collection, Archives, The Sage Colleges.

of bills to develop Florida's rivers and harbors, including Port Everglades. RBO was defeated for a third term in 1932 in part because of her continued support of prohibition.

President Roosevelt appointed RBO as Envoy Extraordinary and Minister Plenipotentiary to Denmark and Iceland in 1933. She became the first woman to represent the U.S. as a minister and the second female diplomat in the world. (Madame Alexandra Kotlantay, Soviet Minister to Norway, was the first, having been appointed to her post in 1923.)

RBO continued as Minister to Denmark until 1936 when she resigned after her marriage to Captain Borge Rhode of the Danish Royal Guards. The wedding took place in Hyde Park, New York, with the President and Mrs. Roosevelt in attendance. After her resignation, the Rhodes moved to Ossining, New York and RBO resumed her career as a public speaker.

President Roosevelt named her as a special assistant to the State Department in 1945, where she helped draft the United Nations Charter. President Truman appointed her as an alternate delegate to the UN General Assembly. RBO also had extensive volunteer involvement in a long list of civic, church and educational organizations.

Ruth Bryan Leavitt Owen Rhode died of a heart attack in Copenhagen on July 26, 1954. She had been in Denmark to receive a medal from the King and was buried in Copenhagen. Her survivors included her husband Borge Rhode and three of her four children.

Edna St. Vincent Millay, B.A.

DOCTOR OF LETTERS-1933

Pulitzer Prize Winning Poet, Author, Pianist, Actor, Songwriter

Edna St. Vincent Millay (1892-1950), known to family and friends as Vincent, was an icon of American letters who first achieved recognition as a published poet when she was fourteen. By her twenties, she had earned national recognition with publication of *Renascence* in the 1912 edition of the anthology *The Lyric Year.*

Miss Caroline Dow, Dean of the New York Y.W.C.A. training school, heard her recite *Renascence* at the Whitehall Inn in Camden, Maine in 1912. Impressed, Dean Dow launched an effort to secure funding for Millay to attend Vassar. After working to fill in gaps in her educational background, Millay enrolled in Vassar, earning her bachelor's degree in 1917.

Millay was both a popular poet and a public poet and published her work in many forms; books, pamphlets, magazine articles, and newspaper articles. Millay was an activist who used her poetry and the public platform provided by newspapers such as the *New York Times*, the *Herald Tribune*, and the *Daily News* to support her positions. Sometimes her public support of a cause was not viewed favorably, as had happened when she was in support of a reprieve for two Italian immigrants, Nicola Sacco and Bartolomeo Vanzetti. In 1920 Sacco and Vanzetti were sentenced to death for murder after a highly controversial trial. Millay was arrested for demonstrating for their reprieve in 1927.

A fierce individualist and feminist, Millay was talented in many areas. She was an accomplished pianist and actress, a playwright, a songwriter, a composer of sonnets, a translator, and a writer of satire and short stories. She wrote under both her own name and that of Nancy Boyd. Her writings as Nancy Boyd were primarily prose pieces submitted to the popular press in her early career to support herself. Millay had a sense of humor, once writing a piece endorsing a work of Nancy Boyd as someone familiar with Boyd's work. Millay spoke six languages and was a sought after lecturer. She was awarded the Pulitzer Prize for Poetry in 1923 for her work, "The Ballad of the Harp-Weaver." She was the first woman to receive the Pulitzer Prize for Poetry.

Also in 1923, Millay married Eugen Jan Boissevain in an open marriage that was unusual for the time. Two years later they purchased property in Austerlitz, New York converting it into a sanctuary where Millay could work and they could play with their many friends. In many ways they transported the bohemian lifestyle of the Jazz Age with a play hard and work hard philosophy from Greenwich Village and Provincetown to an idyllic rural setting. Gradually, Boissevain shifted his focus from his successful coffee import business to taking care of Millay's needs so that she could devote herself to her writing. His devotion and care allowed her the room to write. Her experiences, including her multiple affairs with both sexes and her connections to nature, were the basis of her poetry.

Millay visited RSC three times, twice to read her works. The third time, on June 5, 1933, the degree of Doctor of Letters was conferred on Edna St. Vincent Millay by Russell Sage College. The citation for her degree stated the following:

"Free, vital, winsome, self-reliant poet that you are, you, have taken over, with supreme artistry that is all your own, the English sonnet and have made of it an effective means of composing with precise and measured beauty the songs that the souls of us all have loved to sing. And in so doing you have shown us anew the beauty in truth and the truth in beauty."

"Blending as you have, the daintiness of Queen Anne's lace with the rugged strength of the sturdy oak, the heights of ecstasy, with the valleys of despair, the solemnity of death and war with the levity of figs and thistles, you have written imperishable verse which will remain everlasting proof of the fallacy that true art can never be popular. Posterity would rebuke us if we did not include you in our list of notable twentieth-century women upon whom we confer our highest academic honors."[15]

Although a pacifist during WWI, she, like others, came to a different view following a series of brutal German assaults during 1939-1940. In 1940 she published "Lines Written in Passion and in Deep Concern for England, France, and My Own Country" in three New York City newspapers; the *New York Times,* the *Herald Tribune,* and the *Daily News.* It was widely republished across the United States and Canada, but her call to arms with an end

---

[15] Ibid.

to U.S. isolationism was not popular. Millay retitled the poem, "There Are No Islands Any More," and published it as a pamphlet with proceeds going to the Red Cross or other war relief agencies.

Despite Millay's heavy travel schedule and somewhat fragile health, she was a prolific writer who also maintained correspondence with many literary figures of her time. Her public readings were very well attended. In 1943 Millay was awarded the Frost Medal for her lifetime contribution to American Poetry. Her husband died in 1949 of cancer. Edna St. Vincent Millay died at her Steepletop home following a fall on October 19, 1950.

Annie Warburton Goodrich

DOCTOR OF LAWS-1936

Pioneer in Clinical and Academic Nursing

Annie Warburton Goodrich (1866-1954) was a pioneer in the clinical and academic aspects of nursing. At the age of twenty-four, she entered the New York Hospital Training School for Nurses. In *Her Journey to Yale* (Macmillan, 1950), Esther A. Werminhaus stated that Goodrich compared her preparation for hospital training as analogous to beginning a prison sentence. At that time, nursing education consisted of twelve-hour shifts filled with duties that could not be completed within the time frame, no matter how rapidly the students worked. There were a few lectures given in the off-duty hours and the training lasted only two years. Head nurses were merely senior students who did not receive training on how to teach the younger, first-year students.

In her first year Goodrich made notes on how nursing education could be improved, and how to advocate for changes that would improve the lives of nursing students, nurses, and patients. When she became the Superintendent of Nurses at Saint Luke's Hospital in 1900, she began to implement these changes. One was to alter the assignment of a nurse from a group of specified duties to be carried out for all patients, to a patient-centered approach where each nurse was given responsibility for the complete care of a group of patients. In her opinion, the former led to an emphasis on efficiency at the expense of fundamental therapy.

Goodrich also advocated for increased classroom instruction and clinical training for nurses. She worked for better working conditions for nurses and students, including housing that was close to the hospital. Accessible housing made it easier for the student nurses to attend classes when they were off-duty. By 1900 hospital-based nursing programs were expanding to three years to accommodate the educational changes.

The American Society of Superintendents of Training Schools for Nurses (ASSTSND) was founded in 1893 as a means to establish and maintain a universal standard of training for nurses. It was later renamed the National League for Nursing Education (NLNE). After merging with the National

Organization for Public Health Nursing and the Association for Collegiate Schools of Nursing in 1952, the combined group was named the National League for Nursing (NLN). Goodrich became associated with ASSTSND/NLNE early in its inception and was elected chair of the committee on hospital economics and served in that role from 1904-1913.

A concern of many was the uneven quality of nursing education. Not all states required nurses to register and only New York and Illinois employed inspectors of nurse training schools. In 1912 one estimate was that ninety percent of self-identified nurses had little or no training. Also, there was no law in New York that required a person to have training before being identified as a nurse.

During the Spanish-American War in 1898 there had been a controversy about whether to accept volunteer "nurses" who might not be trained, or to require better-educated, trained nurses. That same controversy resurfaced years later during WWI. A proposal had been made by a Vassar trustee, Mrs. John Wood Blodgett, who approached members of the ASSTSND about funding a program to train volunteer aides during the summer of 1918. She was persuaded instead to fund a program for college-educated women. In June 1917 a letter signed by four nursing leaders was sent to the Presidents and Deans of Colleges for Women and coeducational colleges that outlined a plan for college women to enter nursing programs. Goodrich, President of the American Nurses' Association, was one of the signatories. The plan included a three-month program of pre-clinical study at Vassar during the summer of 1918, followed by a two-year hospital training program. College educated women would then have a training program in nursing of two years and three months.

Advocacy by nursing professionals that began in 1900 for longer hospital training programs had resulted in laws by 1918 requiring three full years of hospital training for nurses in many states. Even those states that did not require the three years adhered to it. As a result, finding training programs that would agree to train the Vassar program graduates for only two years became a problem. Eventually, thirty nursing training programs, including the Connecticut Training School at New Haven Hospital, agreed to enroll the Vassar graduates in a two-year clinical program. Many programs in New York and Massachusetts turned them down because of the legal requirement of a three-year training program. Nursing leaders had come to the realization that the real issue was not the length of training, but the content of the training.

Goodrich was appointed as Chief Nurse Inspector of the Military Hospitals with the Nursing Department of the U.S. Army in 1918, and then as Organizing Dean of the Army School of Nursing. The first class of nurses graduated from the Army School of Nursing in 1921 and it soon became a permanent program.

A few weeks after the Armistice, November 11, 1918, the Rockefeller Foundation hosted a conference of people who were interested in the development of public health nursing in the U.S. and it quickly expanded to address nursing education at all levels. A 585-page report was published in 1923, titled *Nursing and Nursing Education in the United States.* There were ten conclusions in all, but one important directive was that endowed university-based Schools of Nursing must be established if both nursing education and the profession were to grow. A lengthy search for a university to house an independent school of nursing and to secure the endowment for it ensued. There was great support and great opposition to the radical idea of elevating nursing education to the same level as that for other professions like physicians, architects, lawyers, and teachers rather than leaving it as an apprenticeship.

A compromise was worked out and the Rockefeller Foundation proposed a five-year experiment in which a school of nursing would be supported. At the end of the experiment, the program would be evaluated and if deemed successful, an endowment would be provided. Yale University was one of two chosen sites and Goodrich was appointed as the founding Dean of the Yale University School of Nursing. With the support of established innovative nursing programs in New Haven, the faculty of the medical school, and the staff of local hospitals, Goodrich was able to develop policies and programs that became models for other institutions, including Russell Sage College and Albany Hospital.

On June 1, 1936 the degree of Doctor of Laws was conferred on Annie Warburton Goodrich by Russell Sage College, in recognition of leadership "with wisdom, devotion and high vision (in) the onward march of a new profession. . . . a tower of strength in raising nursing from its lowly estate as a domestic occupation to the position, which it now occupies in the highest citadels of our nation."

"It was your outstanding achievement at Yale University which led our two institutions to the belief that there is no movement in education today fraught with greater social significance than the alliance of colleges and hospitals to the end that those who are to be thrown into intimate contact with the painful, tragic, sordid and defective aspects of human life, shall be equipped with more scientific techniques, broader scholarship and a higher vision of the nurse's contribution to a finer social order."[16]

After her retirement from Yale University School of Nursing, she continued to be active in the nursing profession. Goodrich was the Consulting Director of the Nursing Service of the Neuro-psychiatric Institute of the Hartford Retreat from 1938-1941. Annie Warburton Goodrich died in 1954 at the age of 88, and in 1976 she was posthumously inducted into the American Nurses Association Hall of Fame.

---

[16] Ibid.

Winifred Goldring, A.M.

DOCTOR OF SCIENCE-1937

Paleontologist, Educator, Author

Winifred Goldring (1888-1971) earned an A.B. and an A.M. from Wellesley College in 1909 and 1912 respectively. After a short time teaching at Wellesley and in the Boston area, she spent her professional career in Albany, New York. In 1914 John Clarke, the Director of the New York State Museum, hired Goldring as a "Special Temporary Expert in Paleontology." Although Clarke's intent was that Goldring would set up exhibits of fossil invertebrates, she expanded her role to encompass designing and building interpretative exhibits that would inform and engage the viewing public. Her work started with the basics, "What is a Fossil?" and "What is a Formation?" Her exhibit work eventually led to major publications, *Handbook of Paleontology for Beginners and Amateurs (1933)* and *The Guide to the Geology of John Boyd Thacher Park (1933)*. Through multiple printings, these publications served to introduce generations of New Yorkers and others to the rich geologic history of New York State.

Impressed by her work ethic and research skills, Clarke assigned Goldring—still in a temporary position—to review the literature and the museum's unstudied collection of fossil crinoids or sea lilies, in 1916. Two years later Clarke shifted Goldring to a permanent position as an assistant paleontologist. After seven years of work, Goldring published a 670-page monograph that established a systematic classification of fossil crinoids in New York State. This work enhanced her reputation as a professional paleontologist and paleobotanist. Throughout her career, she would reinforce her professional reputation as well as her reputation for making the fossil world accessible to the amateur.

In 1921 Clarke turned to Goldring to study the fossils of Gilboa, New York. New York State had begun to build a reservoir system that would supply fresh water to New York City. Construction of a large dam at Gilboa that would establish one of the feeder reservoirs was begun in 1917. When the dam was completed, the town of Gilboa was obliterated and the surrounding valley was permanently changed. Engineers working on the construction were urged to set aside fossils for scientists. Goldring and her colleague,

Rudolf Reudemann, collected samples from the area until about 1926 when the rising waters in the reservoir stopped the work.

There were few female paleontologists nationally or internationally. Most women who worked at the museum during this time did clerical or support work. It was important to Goldring that she did as much of her own fieldwork as possible at Gilboa, as well as at other sites. As a woman, this presented unique challenges since women would not commonly wear pants for at least another generation. The usual dress for a woman was a voluminous, ankle-length skirt that was unsuitable—even dangerous—for fieldwork, Goldring designed a field outfit of bloomers that were reminiscent of jodhpurs. The outfit was controversial. There were also comments about the "dangerous situations" in which she might find herself, though it was not clear whether the source of danger was animal or human. In any event, Goldring started to carry a revolver when she did fieldwork, although it is not known if she ever used her gun.

Studying the recovered fossils from the dam site, Goldring identified a new genus of fern that she named *Eospermatopteris* (dawn of the seed fern). It was from the Devonian period, about 358 million to 416 million years ago. Since it was a plant transitioning from ferns using spores for reproduction to ones that use seeds, she called them seed ferns. Her designation and terminology persisted for over 80 years. She also designed and constructed an exhibit at the New York State Museum on the Gilboa forest, which made the museum a popular destination for the first time.

On June 7, 1937 the degree of Doctor of Science was conferred on Winifred Goldring by Russell Sage College, in recognition of her professional accomplishments as a paleontologist as well as her educational role in making her professional findings accessible to the public. Her citation included the statement: "By making the plants and animals of prehistoric ages speak to us with intelligible voices today, you are helping us to understand the planetary evolution of our state and to appreciate anew its terrestrial nobility."[17]

Goldring made significant contributions throughout her career, one of which was her study of a series of calcareous concretions in an area near Saratoga Springs, New York. These rounded masses of mineral matter found in sedimentary rock were originally discovered in the 1920s, but there was

---

[17] Ibid.

uncertainty about their origin and nature. Some early researchers thought they were inorganic in origin, others thought they were organic in origin, although they disagreed as to the organic source.

After her characteristically thorough study, Goldring published a report in 1938 identifying three different reefs, each dominated by a different algal species: *Crytozoon proliferium; C. ruedemanni;* or *C. undulatum.* She described the environmental conditions that led to domination by each species in these structures now known as stromatolites. Years later her conclusions were supported by the discovery of living stromatolites under various conditions in Western Australia. The structures in New York were the first to be discovered in North America, but they have now been found and studied in various locations.

Despite accolades and the respect of her colleagues, Goldring briefly resigned from the museum in 1918 because of salary discrimination. Less qualified male colleagues with less responsibility were paid a higher salary, with some male stenographers and clerks paid double her salary. After returning, she remained concerned with the lack of advancement opportunities for women. She encouraged young women to go into scientific fields other than paleontology.

After a provisional appointment as State Paleontologist, Winifred Goldring was appointed as the permanent State Paleontologist in 1939, the first woman to hold such a position in the United States and the highest ranked woman in her field in the world. In 1949 she became the first woman elected President of the Paleontological Society.

Goldring retired as the State Paleontologist at the New York State Museum in 1954. She died in 1971.

Gertrude Vanderbilt Whitney

DOCTOR OF HUMANE LETTERS-1940

Sculptor, Patron of the Arts

Gertrude Vanderbilt Whitney (1875-1942) was born to a family of enormous wealth and position. Her early years followed the pattern of the privileged at the time; home in Manhattan, cottage in Newport, travels abroad, and rounds of dinner parties and balls. Life for young women in these wealthy families was dictated by a set of stringent rules for appropriate behavior. At twenty-one, Gertrude Vanderbilt followed accepted behavior and married Harry Payne Whitney, uniting two large fortunes with the union. She was then expected to assume her social role as Harry Payne Whitney's wife.

Soon after her marriage, Whitney began to seek outlets for her creative nature. She was an avid journal keeper and used her observations to write travelogues. She even tried her hand at writing novels, but soon became aware that her talents were best realized as a sculptor. Over the years, she was taught by prominent sculptors of the time: Hendrik C. Anderson, a Norwegian-American; James Earle Fraser, an American; Andrew O'Connor, an American who lived and worked in Paris for many years. The French pioneer of modern sculpture, Auguste Rodin, even gave her some tips. Whitney had the luxury of money and was able to build studios wherever she needed one.

Whitney also used her wealth to become a Patron of the Arts. She made space available so artists, especially young artists, could exhibit their work. She collected American art and by 1929, she had acquired almost 700 contemporary American works, one of the largest collections of its kind at that time. Whitney thought public exhibition of art was important. Since she no longer had the capacity to exhibit such a large collection, she offered the collection to the Metropolitan Museum of Art. She was also prepared to fund the construction and endowment of a new wing to house the exhibit. Dr. Edward Robinson, the Director, flatly turned down the offer of the collection. Immediately following Dr. Robinson's refusal, Whitney formulated a plan for the Whitney Museum of American Art and it opened in 1931.

When Whitney's husband died in 1930, the fortune she controlled was in the range of $72 million. This vast fortune sometimes caused her problems as an artist. She worked hard to be accepted by her artistic colleagues as an artist, while simultaneously being a benefactor. It was a difficult and precarious position. Sometimes, being the benefactor of an exhibit prevented her artistic work from being exhibited.

Whitney's talent did win her sculpture commissions, however, both in the U.S. and abroad. A few of her public sculptures can be seen today: a fountain sculpture at the Pan-American Building in Washington, D.C. (1909); the *Washington Heights War Memorial* (1921); the *Buffalo Bill Memorial* in Cody, Wyoming (1924); the *St. Nazaire Memorial*, a memorial to the U.S. Army Expeditionary Force who landed at St. Nazaire, France in WWI (1926) and was destroyed by the Germans in WWII and rebuilt in 1989; the *Christopher Columbus* sculpture in Palos, Spain (1929); the *Three Graces* sculpture, McGill University, Montreal, Canada (1930); the *Titanic Memorial* in Washington, D.C. (1931); the *Peter Stuyvesant* statue in Stuyvesant Square (1939); and the *Spirit of Flight*, for the New York World's Fair (1939).

On June 3, 1940 the degree of Doctor of Humane Letters was conferred on Gertrude Vanderbilt Whitney by Russell Sage College, recognizing that she was "an eminent exponent of the art that imparts life to cold stone; a sculptress whose masterpieces of imaginative insight, aesthetic integrity and technical craftsmanship have taught us anew that 'great art is as obvious as the sea and as immeasurable.' " The citation also recognized, "the assistance and encouragement . . . given to the young, struggling, unknown artist, for the gallery you have founded in which all who love art may see with their own eyes its greatest masterpieces . . ."[18]

Active to the end, Gertrude Vanderbilt Whitney died on April 18, 1942 at the age of 67.

---

[18] Ibid.

Eve Curie

DOCTOR OF HUMANE LETTERS-1941

Author, Pianist, Spokesperson for French Women during WWII, UNICEF Activist

Eve Curie (1904-2007) was born in Paris the year after her mother, Marie, and father, Pierre, shared the Nobel Prize in Physics with Henri Becquerel. Before Eve was two years old, her father was killed crossing a Paris street and her paternal grandfather, Eugene Curie, helped care for Eve and her older sister, Irene, so Marie Curie could continue her research. When her grandfather died in 1910, governesses were hired to help with the girls. Marie Curie would go on to win a second Nobel Prize in 1911, this time an unshared prize in Chemistry.

Since money for research was scarce in Europe in the period after WWI, Marie Curie traveled to the United States to solicit funds for her work. Eve, then sixteen years old, and her older sister Irene, accompanied their mother. They acted as both bodyguards and surrogates, filling in for their mother when she was too exhausted to fulfill all her speaking obligations. After returning to Paris, Eve continued her schooling. She graduated from Sévigne College and earned Baccalauréat Général S and L. These degrees have no equivalent in the U.S. education system, but a baccalauréat is required in France to move from secondary education to university studies. She also studied piano, giving her first concert in Paris when she was twenty-one.

Eve continued to care for her mother, often accompanying her on trips, after Irene married. Marie Curie was often ill from what eventually was acknowledged to be the result of her work with ionizing radiation and unshielded x-rays during WWI. After her mother's death in 1934, Eve wrote a well-received biography of her mother, *Madame Curie*. She won the National Book award for her work and the book was adapted and released as a film by M.G.M in 1943.

She wrote for Parisian publications about the theater, music, and movies. She translated the American play, *Spread Eagle*, into French and adapted it for production in France. After the fall of France during WWII, she began to work for the Free France cause and was appointed head of the feminine division of the Commissariat of Information. Eve Curie made seven lecture tours to the United States and gave talks on French women and the War. During one of these tours, Eleanor Roosevelt hosted her at the White House. Curie was an articulate and elegant voice for French women during wartime and became their public voice during WWII.

On June 2, 1941 the degree of Doctor of Humane Letters was conferred on Eve Curie by Russell Sage College, recognizing her as the embodiment of "the indomitable spirit and the superb fortitude of the French people, bound to us by ties that reach back to our nation's cradle and which nothing can ever weaken or break. And we wish to express to you and through you to your fellow countrymen, first, our keen and abiding appreciation of the rich heritage of culture which, during the past ten centuries, you have contributed to western civilization, second, our deepest sympathy in this your hour of suffering and sorrow, and finally our unshakeable conviction that France will rise again in all her greatness and that the tri-color will proudly wave over a people enjoying anew, and in all their glory, those priceless prerequisites to joyous and creative living—liberty, equality and fraternity."[19]

Five months later the *Herald-Tribune* hired Curie to report from anti-Axis territories. She covered approximately 40,000 miles in five months and reported from North Africa, Iraq, Iran, the Soviet Union, Burma, and China. She published a book about her travels, *Journey Among Warriors*, which received mostly positive reviews.

After the war Curie was appointed as the Special Advisor to the Secretary General of the North Atlantic Treaty Organization (NATO), and she served in that role from 1952-54. She resigned from the position in 1954 when she married Henry Richardson Labouisse, an American diplomat and statesman. Labouisse was appointed the second Executive Director of the United Nations International Children's Emergency Fund (UNICEF) in 1965 and would serve in that role until 1979. He accepted the Nobel Peace Prize on behalf of UNICEF while in his first year as Director. Along with her husband, Eve Curie was active on behalf of UNICEF. She continued her work after his death in 1987. In 2005, she was promoted to the rank of 'Officier de la Legion d"Honneur' of the Republic of France, France's highest decoration, for her work with UNICEF.

---

[19] Ibid.

Eve Curie was often identified as the daughter, sister, and sister-in-law of Nobel laureates. Her parents had shared the prize in Physics in 1903 and her mother won the prize in Chemistry in 1911. Eve's sister and brother-in-law, Irene Joliot-Curie and Frederic Joliot, shared the prize in Chemistry in 1935. Eve later pointed out that her mother, sister, and brother-in-law had all died at young ages due to effects of working with radiation. Had her father not been killed in an accident, it is likely that he too would have developed a lethal radiation related disease. Without Eve's talents the stories of these remarkable scientists might have been lost.

Curie became an American citizen in 1958 and died in New York City in 2007 at the age of 102.

Sigrid Undset

DOCTOR OF LETTERS-1941

Author, Nobel Laureate in Literature

Sigrid Undset (1882-1949) was born in Denmark as the oldest of three daughters. Her father was a Norwegian archaeologist with a specialty in the Iron Age, who traveled throughout Europe for his work. Her mother was Danish, spoke multiple languages and was involved in her husband's work. The family moved to Norway when Undset was two years old because her father had to give up fieldwork due to illness. He took a position at the Museum of Antiquities associated with the University of Christiania. As a child, Undset learned archaeology, Norse sagas, and Scandinavian folk songs from her parents. Her father died when she was eleven and his death had a dramatic impact on the family.

Financially, a university education would be out of Undset's reach. After completing middle-school examinations, she took a one-year secretarial course and got a job with a large German company in Christiania (present day Oslo). She worked for the next ten years, helping to support her mother and younger sisters while she wrote at night. Undset's first novel, lengthy and set in medieval Denmark, was rejected for publication. Her next three novels were set in contemporary Christiania and sold well enough that Undset resigned from her secretarial position.

After winning a writer's scholarship, Undset took an extended trip through Europe. In Rome, she met Anders C. Svarstad, a Norwegian painter, and they married in Belgium in 1912. They moved to London for a short time and then back to Rome where their first two children, a son and a daughter, were born. With her third pregnancy, they decided to move back to Norway. Undset moved temporarily to Lillehammer, while her husband readied a house in Christiania. They divorced, however, and Undset remained in Lillehammer where her third child was born.

After her third child—a second son—was born in 1919, Undset returned to the Middle Ages as the setting for her fiction. She started a major project, her trilogy *Kristin Lavaransdatter*, followed by the four-volume *Olav Audunsson I Hestviken*.

She also published a Norwegian retelling of the Arthurian legends. The years between 1919 and 1927 were highly productive from a literary standpoint for her.

In 1928 Sigrid Undset was awarded the Nobel Prize in Literature "principally for her powerful descriptions of Northern life during the Middle Ages."[20] In 1934, Undset published an autobiographical book, *Eleven Years Old,* and also began a new series of historical novels, set in the 1700's. The first volume, *Madame Dorthea,* was published in 1939.

In that same year, WWII broke out and Undset's middle child—a daughter who had been born with developmental problems—died. When Russia invaded Finland in November 1939, Undset donated her Nobel Medal to support the Finnish war effort. When Germany invaded Norway in April 1940 and her older son was killed during the invasion, Undset and her younger son fled Norway. She had been a strong critic of Hitler, and as a result, her books had been banned in Germany. The Nazis used her home as officer quarters during the occupation.

Initially she and her son went to Sweden, but they soon moved to the United States. In the U.S. Undset actively sought aid for Norway and Europe's Jews through writings and public speeches.

On June 2, 1941 the degree of Doctor of Letters was conferred on Sigrid Undset by Russell Sage College, in recognition of her status as "one of the greatest living authors; an historical novelist whose fluent, vivid, convincing prose has turned back the pages of Norwegian history eight hundred years and made us flesh of its flesh and blood of its blood. Because of your distinguished achievement in plowing and sowing and harvesting a period of Norse history which before was only a dark and unknown wilderness, you have become a milestone in the evolution of Scandinavian literature."[21]

Undset remained in the United States and continued to support her country until the end of WWII. Although she returned to Norway after the liberation in 1945, she did not recover from the effects of the war and her exile, never writing another work of fiction or finishing her series set in 1700s.

Sigrid Undset died in 1949 in Lillehammer at the age of 67.

---

[20] The Nobel Foundation, "The Nobel Prize in Literature 1928," accessed February 21, 2014, http://www.nobelprize.org/nobel_prizes/literature/laureates/1928/.

[21] Honorary Degree Collection, Archives, The Sage Colleges.

Women of the Americas:
Twenty-fifth Anniversary–1941

The spring and summer of 1941 was a time of unease in the United States while war was raging in Europe. Public opinion was divided between those who wanted to steer clear of involvement in Europe's conflict and those who thought the United States should come to the aid of those fighting against the Axis alliance. A campaign to achieve equal rights for women led to tension at home between those who thought women still needed some protection and those who thought such protections were paternalistic.

May 27, 1941 was an eventful day at the White House. President Franklin Delano Roosevelt issued a Proclamation of Unlimited National Emergency, one step short of a declaration of war and a degree more ominous than the Proclamation of Limited National Emergency promulgated on September 8, 1939. Roosevelt also addressed the Governing Board of the Pan-American Union and the Canadian Minister at the White House. In his address, Roosevelt stated, "what started as a European war has developed, as the Nazis always intended it should develop, into a world war for world domination. . . . As the President of a united and determined people I say solemnly . . . We reassert the solidarity of the 21 American Republics and the Dominion of Canada in the preservation of the independence of the hemisphere."[22]

An ancillary, but no less important fact was that First Lady Eleanor Roosevelt was an active Honorary Alumna of Russell Sage College. RSC was planning the Twenty-fifth Anniversary of its founding in the fall of 1941 with the theme, "The College Educated Woman and the Future of American Democracy."

According to a letter from Dr. Meader to the RSC faculty on July 22, 1941, the theme of the anniversary was changed at the urging of members of the United States Department of State and the Pan-American Union. The Twenty-fifth Anniversary celebration became a community-based program "dedicated to friendship, understanding, respect and good will among the twenty-one American republics."[23] According to Meader, if the program was successful, the State Department was planning to implement similar programs in other communities across the country.

---

[22] Franklin Roosevelt, "Address before the Governing Board of the Pan American Union," White House, May 27, 1941," Center for the Public Domain and the University of North Carolina, accessed August 2, 2014, http://www.ibiblio.org.

[23] James L. Meader, Letter of July 22, 1941, Archives and Special Collections, The Sage Colleges. Troy, NY.

The celebration ran October 8-13, 1941. There were multiple formal programs, sometimes two or three a day, encompassing various topics including music, art, culture, fashion, economics, labor relations, women's issues, and women's societal roles. Presenters were as diverse as the President of the Argentine Meat Producers Corporation and diplomats from at least five countries.

RSC awarded Honorary Degrees in a ceremony on October 10, 1941 to six prominent women, representative of the Pan-American Union. Eleanor Roosevelt was instrumental in selecting the women to be honored. In most cases she knew the nominees because she had worked with each of them in some capacity. Eleanor Roosevelt wrote the nomination citations and presented the women individually to President Meader during the public ceremony. Celebrating the accomplishments of six women from Republics of the Pan-American Union highlighted the Union and subtly enhanced the status of women throughout the Pan-American Union.

Other events during the week included; a parade, street dancing with Julian Huarte and the Tropicana Orchestra, an exhibition of garments made from Latin-American furs, and displays of Latin-American agricultural products. The Troy and Lansingburgh School Districts, Emma Willard School, the La-Salle Institute, and Rensselaer Polytechnic Institute were among the sponsors of events. Their students and staffs were active participants. Sixty different publishers furnished books on Latin America for a display in Spanish House. In addition, there were exhibits at the Brooklyn (New York) Museum, the Museum of Natural History of New York City, the Museum of Costume Arts in New York City, and various venues in Albany. The amazing cooperation among many diverse groups led to a very full, exciting week.

The events culminated in a Fiesta held in and around Sage Park. Two professional dancers, Lao and Monsita, performed the "Huaka-Tokoris Dance" to a large group gathered before the street dancing. This dance represents one of the leading fertility dances from the Inca Epoch. The elaborate costumes and dance movements highlighted the connection of indigenous people to the earth through symbolism representing bulls, fields, and mountains. The dancers, a male and a female, represented a united effort for a better future. Earlier in the week, Marina Núñez del Prado, one of the Honorary Degree recipients, had exhibited her sculpture, *Danza De Huaka-Tokoris*, an interpretation of the dance sculpted in wood.

Maria Josephina Albano, M.S.

MASTER OF HUMANE LETTERS-1941

Social Worker

Maria Josephina Albano (1916-1995) was born in Fortaleza, Ceará in the Northeast region of Brazil. The family moved to Rio de Janeiro in 1924. Education was important in her family and all were told to prepare to make a living. Albano was educated in Rio de Janeiro, mostly in private Catholic institutions. Originally, Albano was interested in becoming a nurse, but her mother urged her to consider another career. She studied history and geography, but was not interested in teaching. As she was finishing this program, her mother showed her a brochure for a new program in Family Education and Social Work at the Institute Social. Albano was the first student to register. She and three others graduated in the first class from the newly formed Institute Social. The program included both theoretical and practical aspects. While pursuing her degree, Albano worked in the Juvenile Court system. After receiving her degree in 1940, Albano studied English through the Instituto Brasil-Estados Unidos (IBEU.) While at IBEU, she became aware of a scholarship sponsored by the New York Institute of Education to study social work at the New York School of Social Work at Columbia University. She applied and received a scholarship.

On October 10, 1941 the degree of Master of Humane Letters was conferred on Maria Josephina Albano by Russell Sage College, in recognition of her role as a "defender and protector of the dependent, neglected, under-privileged child."[24] Albano was the first student to register in the pioneer school of social work, Institute Social, in Rio de Janeiro. While there, she began a system of guidance for dependent children when they left institutional care. Her thesis, *The Protection of Dependent and Delinquent Children in Brazil,* became a model for social workers in Brazil.

Albano returned to Brazil in January 1943 after earning her Master of Science degree in Social Work from Columbia in 1942. Throughout her career, Albano looked for patterns in the ways that diverse schools of thought and cultures approached similar problems. She adapted what she learned to local

[24] Honorary Degree Collection, Archives, The Sage Colleges.

needs and shared her insights with her colleagues. Albano returned to the U.S. multiple times, especially to learn ways social service agencies interacted with culturally distinct populations, such as Puerto Ricans, and other groups receiving public assistance.

She was active in community work, social infrastructure, organization, and planning, sharing her expertise throughout Brazil and South America. She continued to be active in the Pan-American Union (now the Organization of American States (OAS)), serving as the Chief of the Union of Social Services (1952-1959) that was important in the establishment of the infrastructure for teaching and research in social work in South America. In 1972 she taught at her alma mater, Instituto Social (now known as PUC-RIO), in the first graduate program in Social Work in Rio de Janeiro. Albano's work addressing community development and housing was used in Brazil, Venezuela, Columbia, and Paraguay. Over the course of her career, she always combined her teaching with direct contact with affected populations. She remained sensitive to the local culture as she addressed the broad range of social issues from child protection through urban planning, rural issues, labor issues, housing, community development, and industrial issues.

In 1966, the Conselho Regional de Servico Social named their library after Maria Josephina Rabello Albano in recognition of her pioneering work.

Ester Neira de Calvo

DOCTOR OF PEDAGOGY-1941

Educator, Organizer of the First Inter-American Women's Congress

Ester (aka Esther) Neira de Calvo (1890-1978) was born in Cocle province in the Republic of Panama. She began her education in Panama and continued her studies at the Institut Padagogique de Wavre-Notre Dame in Belgium, at Mount St. Vincent in New York, and at Columbia University in New York. Upon her return to Panama in 1912, she became an advocate for education, women's rights, and social services.

She acquired extensive teaching experience in Panamanian schools from primary through normal schools—those schools for the education of teachers. She became the first woman appointed as the Inspector General of Education (1923-27) and Professor of Education and Director of the only teacher training school for women, Panama's Normal School (1927-1938). To broaden the educational opportunities for women, she founded (1938) and directed (1938-1945) the Lyceum that offered university courses for women. She also advocated for the political and civil rights of women, founding and serving as the president of the National Society for the Advancement of Women in 1923.

On October 10, 1941 the degree of Doctor of Pedagogy was conferred on Ester Niera de Calvo by Russell Sage College, in recognition of her commitment to hold "… high the torch of learning to illuminate, for the youth of your native land, the pathway to a more abundant life."[25] Through education and advocacy, Niera de Calvo urged women to expand their role from the narrow, traditional model of housework only. Building on the National Society for the Advancement of Women, she founded the Patriotic League of Women in 1945. During WWII she coordinated cultural affairs for the Ministry of Education in Panama and supported American troops stationed in Panama.

In 1945 Ester Neira de Calvo and Gumercida Paez became the first two women elected deputies to the Second Constituent Assembly, at which the new Constitution of Panama was written in 1946. Neira de Calvo was instrumental in incorporating protection for minors, children, and women into the

---

[25] Ibid.

constitution. She also authored the laws establishing the Juvenile National Council and the School of Social Service at the University of Panama.

Neira de Calvo was appointed the Panamanian representative on the Inter-American Commission of Women of the OAS in 1939 and served in that role for the next ten years. Subsequently, she was named Executive Secretary of the Inter-American Commission of Women by the Secretary General of the OAS, serving in that role until her retirement in 1965. From 1966-1968 she served as the alternate representative of Panama to the Council of the OAS. This appointment carried the rank of Ambassador.

In 1949, Neira de Calvo moved to Washington, D.C. with her husband, Raul J. Calvo, an official of the Panamanian Government. After his death in 1958, she remained in the city until her death in 1978 at the age of 87. Her papers from her long career as an educator, women's rights advocate, politician, and diplomat are housed at Georgetown University.

Marina Núñez del Prado

MASTER OF HUMANE LETTERS-1941

Sculptor

Marina Núñez del Prado was born in La Paz, Bolivia on October 17, 1912, into a family that encouraged cultural and artistic development. In her teens she studied art at the Academia de Bellas Artes in La Paz. After graduation she was invited to remain at the Academia to teach sculpture and artistic anatomy. She also taught drawing at the American Institute.

After traveling to Argentina, Uruguay, and Peru, Núñez del Prado spent two years living and working in Buenos Aires, Argentina. In 1940 she was awarded a yearlong fellowship from AAUW (American Association of University Women) to study and work in the U.S.

After arriving by boat in New York City in September 1940, Núñez del Prado began an eight-year stay in the U. S. where she produced a series of works, including *Miners in Revolt*, which highlighted the plight of Bolivian miners. The sculpture won a gold medal at an exhibition of the National Association of Women Artists in New York City. In addition to the many sculptures she produced during this time, she was an enthusiastic advocate for education through and in art. She sought to use her art as a means to bring cultures and countries together. Her work continued to draw its inspiration from Bolivia's indigenous Aymara peoples. She sought to foster global and inter-American understanding among women. In appreciation of the fellowship she received from AAUW at an important time in her life, she donated her sculpture *Mother and Child* to the organization. It is now on display at AAUW's national office in Washington, D.C.

On October 10, 1941 the degree of Master of Humane Letters was conferred on Marina Núñez del Prado by Russell Sage College, for her achievements as a sculptor who "working with wood and soil, two substances which play such a large part in the lives of your subjects, you have expressed, with rare insight and consummate skill, both the outer form and the inner spirit of those changeless Indians and Cholos [sic] who for centuries have made their homes in the highlands of your beloved Bolivia."[26] An exhibition of her work was part of the Twenty-fifth Anniversary celebration.

In 1948 Núñez del Prado returned to Bolivia, immersing herself in the music and culture of the indigenous Bolivians. She continued to draw inspiration from travel throughout the Americas and Europe. She exhibited twenty-four of her sculptures at the Venice Biennial in 1952, the first time Bolivia was represented at the exhibition. The next year she visited Pablo Picasso who encouraged her to continue to experiment with her abstractions. Returning to Bolivia, she began to work more with materials native to Bolivia like alabaster, onyx, basalt, *Comanche* granite, and native woods.

Núñez del Prado moved to Lima, Peru in 1972, with her husband, Peruvian writer Jorge Falcón. In Lima, she continued working, utilizing bronze for her larger sculptures. She died in Lima on September 9, 1995. She was buried in her native La Paz, Bolivia.

Marina Núñez del Prado and her four siblings donated the *Caseo Museo Marina Núñez del Prado* to the Bolivian people in honor of their parents, Guillermo Núñez del Prado and Sara Vizearra. The museum houses more than a thousand works of Marina Núñez del Prado, including sculptures, drawings, and sketches. It is the largest collection of her work in the world. Works by her sister Nilda, a goldsmith and painter, are also housed there. There are additional collections of Bolivian silver, colonial and contemporary art, and handcrafts.

---

[26] Ibid.

Ana Rosa de Martínez Guerrero

DOCTOR OF LAWS-1941

Founder of the Federation of Argentine Women, Social Welfare Advocate

Ana Rosa Schlieper de Martínez Guerrero was born in Buenos Aires, Argentina to Enrique Schlieper and Ana Zabalrado on August 15, 1898. She married a wealthy rancher, Guillermo Martínez Guerrero, and they had four children. They were supporters of the democratic tradition and of the important role of women in a democratic movement.

Schlieper de Martínez Guerrero was a founder of an organization, Acción Argentina, formed to defend democracy. She published a fourteen-point list of objectives of the organization and spent several months touring the U.S., giving lectures that stressed the importance of the democratic movement throughout the Americas. It was during this tour that she visited Troy, New York and Russell Sage College.

On October 10, 1941 the degree of Doctor of Laws was conferred on Ana Rosa de Martínez Guerrero by Russell Sage College, in recognition that she was "… one of the truly great women of our day and age. Uniting breadth of culture and marked literary skill to unusual ability as a leader of your sex, you are both prophet and servant of a new ideal for the women of Argentina. . . . It is to such women as you that both continents must look for leadership in promoting respect, understanding and good will among the twenty-one American Republics."[27]

Schlieper de Martínez Guerrero was a prominent practitioner in the social welfare field and a founder of the Federation of Argentine Women. She also served as the head of a group formed to combat Nazi propaganda in Argentina and led a pro-Allies women's group, the Junta de la Victoria during WWII. The group's activities were suspended in 1943 by the pro-Axis Argentine police.

Juan Perón was elected President of Argentina in 1946 and Guillermo Martínez Guerrero was elected to the Argentine Congress the same year. Both

---

[27] Ibid.

Martínez Guerrero and his wife opposed Perón's anti-democratic policies. The organizations in which Schlieper de Martínez Guerrero was active were suppressed and she was sent to jail four times between 1946 and 1953. Her husband was also jailed. He died shortly after his release from prison, as a result of his treatment.

After Perón was exiled, Schlieper de Martínez Guerrero again toured the U.S., declaring that democracy had been restored to Argentina. In addition to her work with the Federation of Argentine Women, she was head of the Association for the Protection of Refugees in Argentina, launching a program to aid refugees. She was also instrumental in setting up a home for the care of older refugees and those with disabilities. In 1965 she was posthumously awarded the United Nations Refugee Agency's Nansen Award for her refugee work.

Ana Rosa Schlieper de Martínez Guerrero died in Buenos Aires on September 4, 1964 of a heart attack at the age of 64.

Concha Romero James, M.A.

DOCTOR OF HUMANE LETTERS-1941

Chief of Intellectual Cooperation in the Pan-American Union

Concha Romero James was born in Chihuahua, Mexico in 1899 or 1900. She moved to California for college, graduating from Pomona College. She also earned a Master's degree in Latin America Studies from Columbia University. In 1933 she moved to Washington, D.C. as a member of the research and editorial staff of the Pan-American Union.

As a staff member of the Pan-American Union, she was a strong advocate for Inter-American cooperation and cultural exchange. She encouraged people-to-people exchanges to bridge barriers of distance, language, and custom. She thought the Mexican people had a unique perspective to offer the Americas. Despite three hundred years of Spanish rule and colonialism with little opportunity for democratic government, Mexico successfully had joined the ranks of independent countries as a strong, modern country.

On October 10, 1941 the degree of Doctor of Humane Letters was conferred on Concha Romero James by Russell Sage College, in recognition that Romero James was "… devoting the most fruitful years of [her] life to the important task of promoting that intellectual and cultural reciprocity which is essential, not only to inter-American understanding and good will, but to the preservation of tolerance, self-restraint and justice which alone can insure the freedom of men's minds and souls."[28] She spearheaded programs to increase greater intellectual cooperation between Mexico and the United States. As Chief of the Division of Intellectual Cooperation in the Pan-American Union, she was instrumental in the organization of Latin-American studies programs in American universities.

In 1952 Romero James left OAS (formerly the Pan-American Union) to work at the Library of Congress as a reference specialist in the Hispanic Division. She was a contributing editor for the Handbook of Latin American Studies, prepared by the Library of Congress. In 1963 she became the Assistant Cultural Attaché at the Mexican Embassy, retiring in 1970. Romero James died at the age of 87 in Washington, D.C.

---

[28] Ibid.

Graciela Mandujano

DOCTOR OF HUMANE LETTERS-1941

*Fostered Improvement in the Standards of Living, Education,
and Agricultural Production in Chile*

Graciela Mandujano was sent in 1915 to the Second Pan-American Scientific Congress in Washington, D.C. as one of thirty-four women among 2,566 participants. She attended sessions where she heard presentations about pan-americanism and internationalism from the perspective of feminists like Jane Addams. Mandujano contributed a paper on language training in Chilean schools. After the meeting, she stayed in the U.S., attending school at Barnard, and working as an editorial assistant at *Pan American Magazine*. She returned to Chile in 1920, bringing "foreign" ideas and connections with her. After her return, Mandujano became an active member of a small feminist group.

One of the ideas Mandujano brought back from her stay in the U.S., was a new attitude toward physical activity. Mandujano worked to convince women from across the economic spectrum that there were benefits to being physically active. Wealthy women were encouraged to improve their health by incorporating physical activity as part of their leisure time. Working-women were shown that physical activity was a way to relieve the pressures of hard work, particularly of repetitive, often tedious tasks. Mandujano did not think that women of any class were taking advantage of the beautiful parks available in Chile.

In Chile, Mandujano gave talks about her observations of her time in the U.S. and compared what she learned to what was happening in Chile. She changed her attitude toward the mill girls sitting outside in the heat of summer and the cold of winter. Previously, she had blamed their disheveled, dirty appearance, and lack of ambition on themselves. Then Mandujano remembered that through cooperative struggles, factories in New York provided rest rooms, lunchrooms, and other amenities for workers, all of which had a ripple effect leading to healthier, happier workers.

Mandujano started looking beyond appearances and encouraged others to do the same. By noticing those who were hidden or ignored, change could be brought. Awareness could lead to changes that were compatible with Chilean culture. In 1935 Mandjuano and others joined together to found the Movement for the Emancipation of Chilean Women (MEMCh), a group that pledged "… to fight for the legal, economic, and reproductive emancipation of women and to involve them in public life to improve their social conditions."[29] Mandujano was particularly involved in outreach to women and children of rural Chile. She began to ask them what they needed, rather than imposing what others thought they needed.

In 1941 Mandujano attended the International Labor Organization (ILO) conference at Columbia University as a Chilean government advisor. While in New York, she visited RSC.

On October 10, 1941 the degree of Doctor of Humane Letters was conferred on Graciela Mandujano by Russell Sage College, in recognition of her contributions to improve the standards of living, education and agricultural production in Chile. In her work as the Assistant Director of the Institute for Rural Education and Chief of the Division of Home Industries of the Department of Agriculture, she demonstrated "breadth of vision, humanity of spirit and patient zeal."[30]

Returning to Chile, Mandujano continued her outreach especially to rural populations, using her contacts in the U.S. to help build a foundation in Chile upon which many programs could be built.

═══════════════════════════

From all accounts, the Twenty-fifth Anniversary Celebration with its emphasis on the twenty-one American republics was successful. It is not known if the State Department was able to use it for a model to be copied in other communities. The Japanese bombed Pearl Harbor two months later and America went to war. Therefore, it is unlikely that the experiment was repeated.

---

[29] Corinne A. Pernet. "Chilean Feminists, The International Women's Movement, and Suffrage, 1915-1950." *Women Suffrage: The View from the Pacific* 69 (2000) 663-688. Accessed September 15, 2015. http://www.jstor.org/stable/3641229.
[30] Ibid.

Katharine Burr Blodgett, Ph.D.

DOCTOR OF SCIENCE-1944

Physicist, Inventor, First Woman Research Scientist Hired at General Electric

Katharine Burr Blodgett (1898-1979) was a physicist and physical chemist who spent most of her career as an industrial chemist at General Electric (GE). Born in Schenectady, New York shortly after her father was killed during a home burglary, she spent her early years in New York City, France, and Germany.

Her interest in mathematics and science was encouraged during college at Bryn Mawr in Pennsylvania where she earned her bachelor's degree in 1917. During a school vacation, she visited the GE laboratories and made the acquaintance of the Assistant Laboratory Director, Dr. Irving Langmuir. Langmuir had known her father, George Blodgett, Director of the Patent Department at GE. Impressed by Blodgett's aptitude and attitude, Langmuir suggested she get a master's degree before seeking employment at GE.

Following Langmuir's advice, Blodgett earned an M.S. in Physics from the University of Chicago in 1918. Her thesis, done under the tutelage of Harvey B. Lemon, involved the chemical structure of poison gas adsorption materials to be used in gas masks, an important area of research during this time of WWI. When she completed her master's, Langmuir hired Blodgett as an assistant in his laboratory. At twenty years old, she became the first woman research scientist hired at GE. She also gained a valuable mentor and colleague in Dr. Langmuir.

While at GE, Blodgett worked with Langmuir in the area of electric current flow under restricted conditions. She also began collaborating with him on his work on monomolecular films on water, part of which led to the awarding of the 1932 Nobel Prize in Chemistry to Langmuir, the first industrial chemist so honored.

After six years in his laboratories, Langmuir arranged for Blodgett to study with the Nobel laureate, Sir Ernest Rutherford, at Cambridge University. Her independent work was in the area of gaseous electronics. She earned her Ph.D. in Physics in 1926, the first woman to earn a Ph.D. in Physics from Cambridge.

Blodgett returned to GE and her collaboration with Langmuir. She continued the work in gaseous electronics, a study that became foundational to the development of plasma physics, the fourth state of matter. They also continued work on monolayer films, Blodgett expanding the work in two significant ways. She used a soap, barium stearate, to successively build the thickness of the film to forty-four molecules, binding it to glass. It turned out that a depth of forty-four molecules allowed the reflection of the film to cancel the reflection of the glass. Thus in 1939 she had invented nonreflecting glass. This led directly to modifications that allowed virtually all modern lenses to have a non-reflective coating permanently adhered to the glass. She also developed a simple color gauge to determine the thickness of thin films. Blodgett obtained six patents for her work in this field. In honoring their close collaboration, the apparatus developed for studying monolayers on water is known as the Langmuir-Blodgett trough. The general area of thin films is sometimes known as Langmuir-Blodgett technology.

On May 14, 1944 the degree of Doctor of Science was conferred on Dr. Blodgett by Russell Sage College, in recognition of her work in developing non-reflective glass. Her mentor and collaborator, Dr. Langmuir, was quoted in her citation as characterizing her as someone having a "rare combination of theoretical and practical ability . . . that is living proof that a woman can be as good a scientist as a man."[31] The citation went on to elaborate that her "discoveries . . . have increased the efficiency of lenses—in aerial cameras and submarine periscopes—have given clear vision to our defenders of Democracy 'in the Heavens above' and 'in the waters beneath the earth.'"[32]

During WWII, Blodgett and Langmuir developed improved protective smoke screens and a method for deicing aircraft wings. Although they continued to collaborate, over time they pursued different areas of research.

Blodgett's contributions to science and industry were often eclipsed by her collaboration with Langmuir. *Science* published an article in 1973, celebrating the seventy-fifth anniversary of the founding of the GE laboratory, but her name was not even mentioned. Her gender made it easier to ignore her scientific contributions. The interactions and collaboration between Langmuir and Blodgett continued until Langmuir's death in 1957. Blodgett

---

[31] Ibid.
[32] Ibid.

continued working on thin films at GE until her retirement in 1963.

From all accounts she led a full and happy life, despite her lack of recognition. She was admired and respected in and out of the laboratory and was especially remembered for her ability to explain complex chemical phenomena in clear, precise language. She died at her home in Schenectady in 1979.

Dorothy Constance Stratton, Ph.D.

DOCTOR OF HUMANE LETTERS-1945

First Full-time Dean of Women at Purdue, First Woman of SPARs, First Director of Personnel at the International Monetary Fund, Executive Director of the GSA

Dorothy Constance Stratton (1899-2006) was born in Brookfield, Missouri at the end of the nineteenth century. Her family moved throughout the Midwest during her childhood. She earned a B.A. from Ottawa University in Kansas. Over the next several years, she taught high school, earned an M.A. in Psychology (University of Chicago), and a Ph.D. in Student Personnel Administration (Columbia University.)

In 1933 Stratton joined the staff of Purdue University as an Assistant Professor of Psychology and the Dean of Women. President Edward C. Elliott of Purdue had started an initiative to increase opportunities for women at the university. This included increasing the number of teaching faculty who were women and expanding the opportunities for female students in fields other than home economics. When Stratton was appointed the first full-time Dean of Women, there were about 500 women students, most majoring in Home Economics. During her nine-year tenure as Dean, she spearheaded development of curricula that made women more welcome and she was able to get three residence halls for women constructed on campus. At the end of her term as Dean, the number of female students had increased to over 1,400. In 1940, two years before the end of her term, Stratton was promoted to full professor.

Stratton took a leave of absence from Purdue in June 1942 to join the military. She was commissioned as a Second Lieutenant in the Women's Reserve of the U.S. Naval Reserve (WAVES) and attended the first class of the U.S. Naval Training Station at Smith College. After training, she was assigned as Assistant to the Commanding Officer of the enlisted WAVES radio school in Madison, Wisconsin. After President Roosevelt signed an amendment to Public Law 773, which created a women's reserve program for the Coast Guard, Stratton became the first woman to be accepted for service. She was named Director of the Coast Guard's Women's Reserve on November 24, 1942 and promoted to Lieutenant Commander.

Stratton suggested the name *SPARs* for the Women's Reserve. She took the name from the Coast Guard Motto, "*S*emper *P*aratus" and its English translation, "*A*lways *R*eady." In her naming memo, she suggested the women would be in a supporting role, analogous to the support supplied by a spar and her suggestion was accepted. As the founding Director of the SPARs, Stratton was responsible for the design and implementation of policies governing women in the Coast Guard service. Stratton developed policies for procurement, training, utilization, and morale of SPARs recruits. She oversaw the growth of the SPARs program to include over 10,000 enlisted and 1,000 officers. These women served their country and freed men for combat positions.

On May 20, 1945 the degree of Doctor of Humane Letters was conferred on Dorothy Constance Stratton by Russell Sage College, in recognition of "her great talent for leadership in the peaceful halls of education and in the service of her country in time of strife." The nominating petition written by Lillian Gilbreth, noted that Stratton's "great capacity for leadership is balanced by her willingness to accept leadership. She believes in and practices the democratic process. Her philosophy of life, her gift for discerning essentials, her sense of humor, her genius for friendship, and her generosity of spirit are qualities which Russell Sage College is proud to honor."[33]

In 1946 SPARs was demobilized and Stratton resigned from the military. For her service, she was awarded the Legion of Merit Medal. Stratton went on to serve as the first Director of Personnel at the International Monetary Fund from 1946-1950. She then became the National Executive Director of the Girl Scouts of America (GSA) until her retirement in 1960. She also served as the United Nations representative of the International Federation of University Women and as the Chair of the Women's Committee of the President's Commission on Employment of the Handicapped.

While Executive Director of Girl Scouts of America, Stratton and Helen B. Schleman, Dean of Women at Purdue University, solicited questions about proper daily social interactions from students at coeducational colleges throughout the country. They published questions and answers in an etiquette

---

[33] Ibid.

manual for postwar "young moderns," titled *Your Best Foot Forward.*[34]

Dorothy Constance Stratton died on September 17, 2006 at the age of 107. On July 28, 2010, First Lady Michelle Obama christened the United States Coast Guard Cutter, USCGC Stratton, in honor of Dorothy Stratton.

---

[34] McGraw-Hill Book Company, Inc., 1955.

Florence Ellinwood Allen, LL.B.

DOCTOR OF LAWS-1947

Musician, Suffragette, Teacher, Attorney, Author, Federal Judge

Florence Ellinwood Allen was born March 23, 1884 in Salt Lake City, Utah Territory to Clarence Emir and Corinne Tuckerman Allen. Florence Allen's maternal ancestors originated in Holland, but were banished for making inflammatory speeches against the ruling monarchy. They moved to England, became Puritans and then sailed to America aboard the Mayflower. By 1812 they had traveled by covered wagon to settle in the Ohio Territory. As they journeyed from Holland to Ohio, they carried with them rhubarb from their Holland home. Over the years, the rhubarb plants became a symbol of the attachment people have to treasured things.

Florence Allen's paternal side also had its roots in New England. Allen's father, Clarence, was a descendant of Ira Allen, active in the Revolutionary War and in New England politics. Ira's brother was Ethan Allen of the Green Mountain Boys fame. Clarence Allen was a Classics professor who also pitched the first curve ball in Ohio. Physicists would come and watch him pitch to study this phenomenon.

In the 1880s Clarence Allen became severely ill from tuberculosis and was advised to move from Ohio to Utah for his health. He taught at Hammond Hall in Salt Lake City as he regained his health. After six years, Clarence Allen resigned from the school and moved his family to Bingham, Utah where he went into the mining business, learning as he worked. He taught himself the science needed for assaying ore and began to work as a mining engineer. He took up law, passed the bar exam, and successfully ran for the territorial legislature. As a legislator, he incorporated important labor reforms for the miners, such as workers' compensation, an eight-hour day, and a six-day week with Sundays off. He also supported legislation to found a free school system.

By 1890 the citizens of the Utah Territory had given up their public support for polygamy and begun the process of seeking statehood. Clarence Allen participated in the convention to write Utah's first state constitution. Included in that constitution was women's suffrage. Once Utah was awarded statehood in

1896, Clarence Allen won election to Congress as a Utah representative with voting privileges. Prior to being granted statehood, the Utah representative was a nonvoting member of Congress. Clarence Allen served in Congress from 1896-1897. He declined to run for a second term, returning to his mining career.

Both paternal and maternal sides of the family valued education and, even more remarkable for the times, equal educational opportunities for women. Florence Allen's mother, Corinne, was in the first class at Smith College. Corinne Tuckerman dropped out in her junior year to marry Clarence Allen, but she always considered herself a "Smith Girl", as did the college. She eventually finished her degree at Grand River Institute in Ohio.

Corinne Allen belonged to the group of first generation, college-educated American women. These women took the lead in a variety of endeavors. Corinne Allen was an activist in women's reform groups and took active roles in various organizations that focused on the lives of women, mothers, children, and workingwomen, even as she raised her family of seven children. She was a charter member of the Daughters of the American Revolution (DAR) founded in 1890 in protest of the exclusion of women from the Sons of the American Revolution organization. Corinne Allen was responsible for instilling a love of classical music in Florence Allen, even having a piano shipped to Utah, not an easy task in those days.

The efforts of both of Allen's parents in furthering the rights of women led to an invitation for Corinne and Clarence Allen to speak at the National American Woman Suffrage Association convention in 1896. Susan B. Anthony introduced them to the audience. According to Tuve, Allen regretted that her parents did not live to see many of her successes. "It was their image, their sense of morality, justice and civic responsibility that sustained her for a lifetime."[35]

One of Florence Allen's earliest memories was learning to read Greek from her father. Throughout her life, she relaxed by reading classics in the original Greek and Latin. While her father was in Congress, Florence and her two older siblings moved in with family in Ohio and attended school. In 1900 Florence Allen enrolled in the Women's College of Western Reserve, was elected to Phi Beta Kappa in her junior year, and graduated in 1904. After graduation Florence Allen accompanied her mother and five siblings to Berlin, where her

---

[35] Jeanette E. Tuve, *First Lady of the Law*. Lanham, MD: University Press of America, Inc., 1984, p.9.

mother was giving a talk at a meeting of The International Council of Women. They stayed for two years. In Germany Allen studied piano with the intent of becoming a concert pianist, but a nerve injury derailed that plan. During this time she also worked as a music critic and correspondent. Allen did not like the Prussian way of life and returned to Ohio in 1906.

For several years Allen taught at the Laurel School for girls in Cleveland and worked as a music critic and columnist for the Cleveland Plain Dealer. She also earned a master's degree in political science and constitutional law from Western Reserve in 1908, and decided to pursue law as a career. Although her first choice for law school was Western Reserve, they did not accept women students in their professional schools, so she became one of four women enrolled in the incoming class of the University of Chicago Law School. Allen did not like the way the courses were taught, so left and moved to New York City to work as a social worker for the League for the Protection of Immigrants and the Henry Street Settlement. When she decided to go back to law school, she began taking night classes in the New York University Law School. Her first choice in New York City was Columbia Law School, but like Western Reserve, they did not accept women students. When she left social work to enroll full-time in law school, she worked at the National College Women's Equal Suffrage League to pay her bills.

During the 1912 summer break from law school, Allen went back to Cleveland to campaign for Amendment Twenty-three to the new Ohio constitution. This amendment eliminated "white male" and substituted "every citizen" in the section on voting requirements. During that summer, Allen made ninety-two speeches throughout Ohio urging acceptance of the amendment. The amendment was defeated.

Allen returned to New York City in the fall and completed her last year of law school, graduating in 1913. She passed the Ohio bar exam and returned to Cleveland. She was unable to secure a position in a law firm, so she opened her own law office in 1914. Eventually she combined offices with other young lawyers who were also starting out. She had met the other lawyers while volunteering for the Cleveland Legal Aid Society.

Allen continued working for the equality of women. When she passed the bar in Ohio, the Ohio Bar Association welcomed her as a member, although the American Bar Association prohibited women members until 1918. She was a member of both the National Association of Women Lawyers (NAWL) and the National Federation for Business and Professional Women's Clubs (NFBPWC). NAWL and NFBPWC were among the most influential organizations that supported Allen throughout her career.

From 1919-20 Allen gained experience serving as assistant county prosecutor for Cuyahoga County, Ohio. This gave her insight into some of the strengths and weaknesses of the court system. It also marked one of her "firsts" in the judicial system as the first woman to hold an office as a county prosecutor.

After ratification of the Nineteenth Amendment in August 1920, Allen declared her candidacy for Judge of the Cuyahoga County Court of Common Appeals. Prior to the passage of the Nineteenth Amendment, women were not able to either vote or hold elective office. Within weeks of the passage of the Nineteenth Amendment, Allen was elected. She credited part of her success to the name recognition she had with voters, especially women voters, earned while campaigning for women's suffrage.

Upon her election the other judges, all male, suggested that a separate divorce court be opened with Allen as the presiding judge. Allen refused because she did not want to be relegated to domestic affairs. She also suggested that of all her fellow judges, she was the least qualified to judge domestic affairs, since unlike each of them she was not and had not been married. The suggestion to have a separate divorce court quietly went away.

Two years later, Allen ran for and won a seat on the Ohio Supreme Court by a wide margin. This 1922 election led to another first. Allen became the first woman to serve on the court of last resort of any state.

During her time sitting on the courts in Ohio, Allen presided over a wide range of cases and increased the efficiency of the courts. She also led reforms that increased the fairness of the proceedings. She addressed the issue that arose when the accused in a case could be free on bond while a victim of a crime could be held in protective custody, often for months as delays occurred. The victim would be separated from his or her family, often with a job loss. In the meantime, the accused might be free, perhaps after posting a bond. Through her efforts, the delays were reduced dramatically.

Allen served on the Ohio Supreme Court until 1934 when President Franklin

D. Roosevelt appointed her to the U.S. Court of Appeals for the Sixth Circuit. She was the first woman to sit on any federal bench of general jurisdiction.

In the twenty-five years that Allen sat on the Sixth Circuit Court of Appeals, she was involved in and wrote opinions for major cases. One of the most important occurred early in her tenure (1938) when as the presiding judge of a three-judge panel, she wrote the opinion that established the constitutionality of the Tennessee Valley Authority Act. Her opinion was appealed to the U.S. Supreme Court and was upheld. Shortly before her retirement, Allen was named Chief Judge of the U.S. Court of Appeals in 1959. Again, this was a first for a woman. Allen retired later that year at the age of 75.

On June 1, 1947 the degree of Doctor of Laws was conferred on Justice Allen by Russell Sage College, in recognition that Allen had been "… a pioneer woman in [her] profession of the Law, and as one who fearlessly and successfully opened doors heretofore closed to women. … [and] the best known woman lawyer in the world."[36]

Advocates, including Eleanor Roosevelt, encouraged Presidents Franklin Roosevelt, Truman and Eisenhower to appoint Allen to the Supreme Court. Although all agreed her qualifications were excellent, each of the presidents concluded that because women voters did not vote as a bloc, there was no political advantage to nominating the first woman to the U.S. Supreme Court. Some of the objections voiced, such as no bathrooms for women or that having a female justice would interfere with a (male) justice being able to relax, were the same objections raised many years later when Sandra Day O'Connor became the first woman appointed to the U.S. Supreme Court. Associate Justice Ruth Bader Ginsburg has written about the important role that Florence Ellinwood Allen played in being a trailblazer for women in the federal judiciary.

Florence Ellinwood Allen wrote during court recesses, publishing *This Constitution of Ours* (1940) and *The Treaty as an Instrument of Legislation* (1952). Her memoir, *To Do Justly* (1965) is an interesting account not only of all her firsts, but also of her reaction to the stresses and disappointments of being the "first" so often. Throughout her life, she continued in advocacy roles, especially for women.

Florence Ellinwood Allen died in Waite Hill, her Ohio home, on September 12, 1966.

---

[36] Honorary Degree Collection, Archives, The Sage Colleges.

Georgia Neese Clark, B.A.

DOCTOR OF HUMANE LETTERS-1950

First Woman Treasurer of the U.S., Actress, Banker, Business Executive

Georgia Neese (1898-1995) was born to a prominent family in Richland, Kansas. At the time of her birth, her father was the town's leading citizen, owning much of the property in town as well as the bank and general store. Neese graduated with a bachelor's degree from Washburn University in Topeka, Kansas as an economics major and drama enthusiast. Following graduation, she moved to New York City to attend Sargent's Dramatic School.

After two years at Sargent's, she began a career as an actress in traveling stock companies. She married her manager, George M. Clark, in 1929 and though the marriage ended in divorce, she would be known throughout her professional life as Georgia Neese Clark.

In 1930 events changed the direction of Clark's life. The deepening Depression and the emerging movie industry made jobs for stage actors scarce. Since Clark was needed to care for her ailing father in Kansas, she gave up her acting career and moved back home.

Following her move, Clark became prominent in the banking and business worlds of Kansas. She had risen from an assistant cashier at her family's privately owned bank, Richland State Bank, to President following her father's death in 1937. She also managed the family's other businesses, like the General Store, a grain elevator, and extensive property.

As her business and banking successes grew, Clark became involved in Democratic Party politics. By 1932, she was a member of the Junior National Committee of the Democratic Party and she actively campaigned for FDR in heavily Republican Kansas. She was named to the Democratic National Committee in 1936, a position she would hold until 1964. Through her work with the Democratic Party, she became a sought after speaker and often shared the podium with other prominent Democratic speakers such as Eleanor Roosevelt, who became a close friend. She also became a close friend and protégé of India Edwards, head of the women's division of the Democratic National Committee.

The women's vote was very important in the election of Harry Truman in 1948. India Edwards, among others, urged Truman to start a "New Deal for Women" and to appoint more women to executive positions in the federal government. Clark's service to the Democratic Party, along with her banking and business experience made her an attractive addition to the list of possible female appointees. When the Treasurer of the United States, William A. Julian, died suddenly, Truman appointed Clark as his successor on June 4, 1949. Five days later, the Senate unanimously confirmed her and she was sworn in as Treasurer on June 21, 1949.

Clark's appointment as the twenty-ninth Treasurer marked the first time a woman became the Treasurer of the United States. It also marked the beginning of a new tradition of female Treasurers; there have been no male Treasurers since her appointment in 1949.

On November 17, 1950 the degree of Doctor of Humane Letters was conferred on Georgia Neese Clark by Russell Sage College, in recognition of her . . . "resourcefulness, strength of inner spirit, and willingness to undertake new ventures which we admire in the national character . . . It gives Russell Sage College great pleasure to honor the first woman Treasurer of the United States, and, at the same time, to express our admiration for Mrs. Clark of Richland, Kansas."[37]

Clark remained Treasurer until January 20, 1953, when President Eisenhower, a Republican, assumed office. Clark returned to Kansas and resumed her business and banking activities. After her marriage in 1953 to Andrew J. Gray, she would be known as Georgia Neese Clark Gray.

Gray resigned from the National Democratic Committee in 1964 after twenty-eight years of service. The same year she moved her family-owned bank to Topeka and renamed it Capital City State Bank. In his obituary of Mrs. Gray, Wolfgang Saxon, quoted President Truman. "Mrs. Gray is the only United States Treasurer since the Civil War who really worked at her job. She knows money affairs as well as any man, and anyone who brings their money here will know it is in charge of someone who knows how to take care of it."[38]

Georgia Neese Clark Gray died at the age of 97 in Topeka, Kansas.

---

[37] Ibid.

[38] Wolfgang Saxon, "Georgia Neese Clark Gray, 95, First Woman as U.S. Treasurer," *New York Times Late Edition East Coast*, October 28, 1995, *ProQuest Historical Newspapers: The New York Times with Index* (430333344). Although the headline states that she was 95, she was 97 when she died.

Elizabeth Gray Vining, M.S.

DOCTOR OF HUMANE LETTERS-1952

Tutor to Crown Prince of Japan, Author

Elizabeth Gray Vining (1902-1999) was born in Philadelphia, Pennsylvania, to a Scottish-born father and a mother from an old Quaker family. Violet, her only sibling, was nineteen when Elizabeth was born. During her childhood, her father suffered business setbacks starting in the recession of 1907. The change in economic status had a profound effect on her older sister's social standing. Elizabeth's upbringing was comfortable, but since she had not known anything different, the change in social status did not impact her as much as it did her sister.

Vining identified herself as an author from a young age. She sold her first work of fiction for two dollars to *The Young Churchman*, a small Episcopal weekly. She was thirteen years old, and her story was titled "The Boys' Revenge." Two years later, she submitted another story for which they paid her three dollars. When she was sixteen, her parents enrolled her at Bryn Mawr, although she preferred to go to college in New England. Immediately after graduation in 1923 with an A.B. degree, Vining went home and began writing in earnest. As rejections piled up, it became apparent to her that she was not going to be able to make a living through writing. She took a job teaching English Literature, Composition, and Community Civics at a New Jersey High School and wrote when the school day was ended. After four and a half months, she decided that teaching was not for her. She enrolled at the Graduate School of Library Science at Drexel Institute. After graduation, she accepted a job in the cataloguing department of the library at the University of North Carolina at Chapel Hill (UNC-CH).

While at the UNC-CH, she met Morgan Vining, a college administrator, and they married in January 1929. As the Depression deepened in 1932, it became obvious that there would be job losses at UNC-CH. Morgan Vining also realized that if he intended to stay in higher education, he needed to earn a Ph.D. With the loss of his job a possibility, they decided it was a good time for him to go to graduate school. They moved to New York City, where Morgan enrolled in the graduate school at Columbia University and

Elizabeth got a job in Columbia's library. With other part-time work and se-
rial apartment sitting, things seemed to work out for them. At the beginning
of their second year in New York City, and four years after they were married,
they were in a car accident on their way to visit Yale University. Morgan was
killed instantly and Elizabeth was severely injured. Coping with her grief and
her lengthy convalescence led her to return to the Quaker meeting of her
childhood and her maternal ancestors. She found solace in their ways and
began to study Quakerism, eventually joining the Society of Friends.

It was during this time that Vining began to write books for children and
young people, traveling abroad to do research for her books. Elizabeth, her
sister Violet, and her mother combined households in Germantown, Pennsylvania to economize and support each other. While her sister worked as a
librarian, Vining took care of her mother and wrote. In March of 1945, she
went to work for the American Friends Service Committee (AFSC) as an
assistant to John Rich of the Publicity Department.

In 1946 after Japan's defeat in WWII, American forces occupied Japan under
the rule of General Douglas MacArthur. Politically, it was a priority to trans-
form Japan from a closed, imperialist society to a more open, democratic
society. A key piece in that transformation was the royal family, especially
the twelve year-old Crown Prince and the future ruler of Japan. It was announced in the *New York Times* that the Emperor wanted an English tutor
for his son. Specific requirements were for an older American woman, who
was a Christian, but not a missionary, and who had an unbiased view of
Japan. Dr. George Stoddard, Superintendent of Education in the State of
New York, was charged with finding a suitable candidate and he was inun-
dated with applications. A colleague of Vining's at the AFSC suggested she
apply, but she declined to apply directly although she said that she would
accept the position if it was offered. Her colleague forwarded her credentials
to Dr. Stoddard, and she was selected to be the Crown Prince's tutor.

There is disagreement, however, about whether Emperor Hirohito or General
MacArthur was the person responsible for selecting Elizabeth Gray Vining
to be the Crown Prince's English language tutor. Vining said that it was
Emperor Hirohito who initiated the idea and the Japanese who made the
decision. Others argue that nothing of consequence happened in post-war
Japan without MacArthur's initiation and/or approval. Regardless of the

locus of approval, Vining had a profound effect on the Crown Prince and the Royal Family. Though she was a citizen of the occupying country, the Japanese government—not the Occupation Administration—employed her. Her gentle approach encouraged the young man in many ways: to become more open, to find his own way, to seek guidance, and not to be afraid of making a mistake.

Her duties expanded to include tutoring of other members of the Royal Family. Vining met with the Emperor and his wife to discuss their son's progress and education and after four years, it was clear that the experiment had been successful. The Japanese government awarded her the Order of the Sacred Crown medal for her work with the Royal Family. Vining returned home and resumed her life as a writer.

On June 1, 1952 the degree of Doctor of Humane Letters was conferred on Elizabeth Gray Vining by Russell Sage College, partly because of her successes as an author of literature for children as evidenced by the Newberry Medal in 1943 and the *Herald Tribune* Spring Festival Prize in 1945. In addition, Vining's appointment in 1946 as a tutor to the Crown Prince of Japan, "held promise of service in the cause of peace for an American biographer and spiritual descendant of William Penn . . . we are less apprehensive of destructive forces in a world in which such teachers are given opportunity to affirm their faith in ways of life that lead to peace."[39]

Vining continued a relationship with the Crown Prince, through letters, phone calls and occasional meetings after she left Japan. She was the only Westerner to attend the royal wedding in Japan in November 1952 and she met the Crown Prince when he came to the U.S. in 1987. In 1994 six years after he ascended the throne, Emperor Akihito made an official visit to the U.S., and Vining was invited to meet with him at the White House. She was forced to decline because of ill health, although she did speak with him in a lengthy phone conversation.

Over the course of her eighty-four-year writing career, Vining wrote many fiction and non-fiction books for both children and adults. She published her books under both her maiden (Elizabeth Janet Gray) and married (Elizabeth Gray Vining) names. In addition to the Newbery Medal for *Adam of*

---

[39] Honorary Degree Collection, Archives, The Sage Colleges.

the Road (1943), she also won the Newbery Honor Medal three times for *Meggy McIntosh* (1931), *Young Walter Scott* (1936), and *Penn* (1939). She wrote an account of her time with the Crown Prince, *Windows for the Crown Prince* (1952) and wrote a sequel, *Return to Japan* (1960) after she returned from the Royal Wedding. She also wrote a memoir/autobiography covering her life to age sixty, *Quiet Pilgrimage* (1970) and a book of daily notes in her seventieth year, *Being Seventy* (1978). Elizabeth Gray Vining died on November 27, 1999 at the age of 97.

Doris Emrick Lee, A.B.

DOCTOR OF LETTERS-1954

Artist, Illustrator, Printmaker, RSC Student

Doris Emrick Lee (1905-1983) was born in a small town in rural Illinois not far from the Mississippi River. Her father, a merchant and banker, and her mother, a schoolteacher, raised six children. A large extended family of two great-grand-mothers, two grandmothers, and many great aunts, uncles and cousins, lived nearby. Her father believed travel was a broadening experience, and he took the large family to California twice for the winter. Her parents made education a priority and a liberal arts college education was a requirement.

Members of her extended family actively engaged in creative endeavors, including painting. Lee recalled her grandfather was a farmer and a "Sunday painter" and Lee, although a self-described tomboy, enjoyed painting and making things like place cards for family dinners. One summer she took painting lessons from a neighbor on her back porch.

The emphasis on a liberal arts education meant that serious painting had to be put on hold to study latin, history, mathematics, and physics at a boarding school in Lake Forest, Illinois in preparation for college entrance exams. In rebellion, Lee cut her hair off. She was suspended for a week and sent home because "nice girls have long hair."[40] Her punishment was to memorize poetry.

Lee began her college career at Russell Sage College, but transferred after her first year (1922-23) to Rockford College in Rockford, Illinois, so that she would have more time to pursue her art. Once enrolled in Rockford College, Lee found her studies less confining. Although she enjoyed mathematics, she wrote in her introductory notes to the American Artists Group collection of her prints, that a "fascinating abstract occupation [mathematics] would swallow up too many of the other things I loved."[41] Her parents would not allow her to attend Art School in lieu of a liberal arts education, so she studied literature and philosophy and took painting classes. She began saving her money so that she could study in Paris after graduation.

---

[40] Doris Lee, *Doris Lee* (New York: American Artists Group, 1946) 2.
[41] Ibid.

She married Russell Lee, an engineer and later a photographer with the Farm Security Administration, in 1927. They honeymooned in Italy and France where Lee studied painting. She also studied painting in Kansas City, San Francisco, New York City, and Woodstock, New York, looking for new experiences and enrolling in formal classes. Some of her stays were brief, others lengthy. As she continued to study and learn, she tried different styles and approaches. Arnold Blanch, one of her teachers in San Francisco, suggested she try painting what appealed to her and from nature. Lee said that advice led her to develop her own style, which made painting less work-like and more fun. As she started to enjoy what she was doing, it was reflected in her paintings and she began to exhibit some of her work.

Lee and Blanch were close personal friends of the artist Milton Avery and his wife Sally. They lived near each other in Woodstock and vacationed together. The Averys are represented in at least one of Lee's paintings, *Florida Vacation*. Lee's use of a combination of abstraction, folk art flattening, and simplification of representational form, shows the influence of Avery on Lee's work. Her paintings also show the influence of Paul Klee, Ben Shahn, Arshile Gorky, and Andre Lhote.[42]

On the same day in 1935, Lee was notified she had won the Logan Prize at the Chicago Art Institute, as well as a commission from the U.S. Treasury Department (Works Progress Administration [WPA]) to do a series of murals for Federal Buildings. The Logan Medal of the Arts was a prize initiated in 1907, named for Frank Granger Logan, a member of the Board of the Art Institute for over 50 years. His wife, Josephine Hancock Logan, strenuously objected to the awarding of the prize to Lee's painting *Thanksgiving* (aka *Thanksgiving Day* and *Thanksgiving Dinner*) because of the style of Lee's work. In response to the award to Lee, Logan founded the conservative Society for Sanity in Art. Lee said that she found the criticism "amusing" and because of Logan's public battle with the Art Institute of Chicago, more people heard of Lee and were exposed to her work. Under the auspices of the WPA, Lee painted two murals in the Main Post Office in Washington, D.C. and one in the Post Office of Summerville, Georgia.

In 1939 Doris and Russell Lee divorced. Doris Lee then married her former teacher Arthur Blanch. Lee would continue to be known as Doris Emrick Lee.

---

[42] Melody Davis, Ph.D., Assistant Professor, Art History, The Sage Colleges, note to the author, December 16, 2014.

On May 30, 1954 the degree of Doctor of Letters was conferred on Doris Emrick Lee by Russell Sage College, in recognition of her ability to ". . . interpret with the artist's insight what might be lost to us in the hurly-burly of twentieth century living – the poetic nature of the ordinary. You show us the charm we might discover for ourselves – did we but look more thoughtfully – in a country wedding or in a Sunday outing. You re-kindle our interest in the scenes in which our lives are set and in so doing, restore our kinship with our fellow men."[43]

In addition to easel work and murals, Lee was a printmaker and an illustrator of books and magazines, particularly for *Life*. She traveled extensively, sometimes on assignment. She did the 1951 cover of the *Rodgers and Hart Songbook* as well as the cover for James Thurber's *The Great Quillow*, and screen designs and sets for Rodgers and Hammerstein's plays. She taught as a guest artist at Michigan State University and the Colorado Springs Fine Arts Center. Her style continued to evolve. In the '60s, her work became abstract meditations on color and form.

Lee's works are part of the collections of many institutions: The Smithsonian American Art Museum; the Art Institute of Chicago; The Metropolitan Museum of Art; The Dayton Art Institute; The Whitney Museum of American Art; and the Albright-Knox Museum.

Lee retired from painting in the late '60s as her health declined. She was diagnosed with Alzheimer's Disease in 1968 and died in 1983 in Clearwater, Florida at the age of 78.

---

[43] Honorary Degree Collection, Archives, The Sage Colleges.

Jacqueline Cochran

DOCTOR OF HUMANE LETTERS-1955

Founder of Jacqueline Cochran Cosmetics, Inc., Pilot, Holder of Multiple Aviation Records, Director of Training for the WASPs in WWII, Recipient of Numerous U.S. and International Air Medals

Jacqueline "Jackie" Cochran (~1910-1980) was a person of distinction, courage and tenacity who lived a fairytale life. Her origins are obscured and lost in the mists of time; even her birth name is a matter of debate as is the source of the name Jackie Cochran. She claimed to pick Cochran out of a Pensacola phone book because she thought it sounded like her name. The specifics of her early life are unknown.

There is agreement, however, that she was born in the rural south in the early part of the twentieth century. Her early years were modest and she had little formal education after dropping out during second grade. From a young age (variously reported as six, ten or thirteen), she worked at a series of unskilled jobs, eventually training as a beautician. She trained for three years as a nurse in a hospital in Montgomery, Alabama and she did well in the practical hands-on aspects, but academically she had difficulty. She never took the State Board Examinations because she was certain she would fail them. However, her nursing training gave her the skills to save Lyndon Johnson's life years later during a medical emergency that occurred while she was secretly flying him from Dallas, Texas to the Mayo Clinic in Minnesota.

Ambitious and driven, Jackie Cochran as she was then known, learned to fly in three weeks in the early 1930s and had a commercial pilot's license within two years. She used air travel to expand her cosmetics business, Jacqueline Cochran Cosmetics, Inc., that she had started with the help of her husband, Floyd Odlum.

Jackie Cochran had found her calling and flying took over her life. She participated in her first major air race in 1934 and won the Bendix Transcontinental Air Race in 1938. She was considered to be the best female pilot in the U.S. and established a new transcontinental speed record. In 1938, she helped design the first oxygen mask with Dr. Randolph Lovelace and she became the first person to fly above 20,000 feet wearing a mask. She established speed records and altitude records.

As a test pilot, Cochran flew and tested the first turbo-supercharger installed on an aircraft engine as well as the first wet wing (sealed wing structures that are used as fuel tanks) installed on an aircraft. She suggested structural modifications of aircraft she tested, leading to new designs and also tested gyro instruments in flight for the Sperry Corporation. In 1941 Cochran became the first woman to pilot a military bomber across the Atlantic, as part of "Wings for Britain" that delivered American built aircraft to Britain.

In 1940 Cochran lobbied Eleanor Roosevelt, Colonel Robert Olds, and General Henry Arnold with a proposal for a women's flying division in the Army Air Force to do domestic, noncombat aviation jobs, thus releasing male pilots for combat. Her proposal was approved in August 1943. The division was named the Women's Airforce Service Pilots (WASPs), and Cochran was appointed the Director of Women's Flying Training.

Cochran set up rigorous requirements and training. More than 25,000 women applied but only 1,830 were accepted and 1,074 graduated. From August 1943 until they were disbanded in 1944, WASPs flew approximately 60 million miles with only thirty-eight fatalities or about one fatality for every 16,000 hours of flight. Cochran was awarded the Distinguished Service Medal for her efforts during the war.

After the WASPs were disbanded, Cochran worked as a press correspondent. She was present at the surrender of General Yamashita, the Japanese Commander in the Philippines. She reported from China, Russia, and Nuremburg, and was the first U.S. woman to enter Japan after the war.

Cochran lobbied for an independent Air Force, which was established as the United States Air Force (USAF) in 1947. In 1948 Cochran joined the USAF Reserve. By the time she retired from the USAF Reserve in 1970, she had risen to the rank of Colonel.

On May 18, 1953, using a borrowed Royal Canadian Air Force jet, Cochran became the first woman to break the sound barrier. Two years later, on May 29, 1955 the degree of Doctor of Humane Letters was conferred on Ms. Cochran by Russell Sage College, "in tribute and salute to the soaring spirit of the child of the sawmill towns that would not be held earthbound."[44] According to her self-generated list of honors, RSC was the first college or university to honor her with an Honorary Degree.

Cochran continued to set firsts: she was the first woman to land on and take off from an aircraft carrier; she set a speed record of 1,429 mph in 1964; and she was the first woman to reach Mach 2. Unfortunately, with the advent of jets, many planes were restricted to the military and off-limits to a civilian pilot like Cochran. Cochran was able to access some planes through her friendship with General Chuck Yeager.

In the 1960s Cochran was a sponsor of the Mercury 13 program that tested the ability of women to be astronauts. Even though the women met or exceeded the results of male astronaut candidates, NASA canceled the program.

Cochran's list of awards was long and extensive. Until she was grounded from flying because of heart problems and implantation of a pacemaker, she held more international speed, distance, and altitude records than any other pilot, male or female. She was awarded the U.S. Distinguished Service Medal, decorated with the French Medal of Honor and the French Air Medal. She was awarded Wings of Air medals from Belgium, Spain, Thailand, Turkey, and pre-communist Rumania. She won the Clifford Burke Harmon International Trophy of the International League of Aviators as the outstanding woman flyer in the world, fifteen times. Jackie Cochran died on August 9, 1980.

---

[44] Ibid.

1929 COMMENCEMENT

l to r Harvey Cowee (Trustee), Eleanor Roosevelt (Honorary Degree Recipient), Eliza Kellas (Honorary Degree Recipient), James L. Meader (President, RSC). Original photograph by Bert Boice of Troy, NY, used with permission of the Archives of The Sage Colleges.

1930 COMMENCEMENT

l to r James L. Meader (President, RSC), Lillian Moller Gilbreth (Honorary Degree Recipient), Edgar H. Betts (Trustee), Ruth Bryan Owen (Honorary Degree Recipient) and Frederick C. Ferry (President, Hamilton College). Used with permission of the Archives of The Sage Colleges.

1933 COMMENCEMENT

l to r Eliza Kellas (former President, RSC), Edna St. Vincent
Millay (Honorary Degree Recipient), Judge Herbert F. Roy
(Trustee). Original photograph courtesy of the Knickerbocker
Press and Mr. Julius Heller, used with permission of the Archives
of The Sage Colleges.

1936 COMMENCEMENT

l to r Fannie French Morse (Honorary Degree Recipient), Annie Warburton Goodrich (Honorary Degree Recipient), James Lukens McConaughy (President of Wesleyan University), Mary Mattingly Meloney (Honorary Degree Recipient) and James L. Meader (President, RSC). Original photograph courtesy of the Knickerbocker Press and Mr. Julius Heller, used with permission of the Archives of The Sage Colleges.

1941 COMMENCEMENT

l to r James L. Meader (President, RSC), Eve Curie (Honorary Degree Recipient), Sigrid Undset (Honorary Degree Recipient) and Emma Perry Carr (Honorary Degree Recipient). Used with permission of the Archives of The Sage Colleges.

TWENTY-FIFTH ANNIVERSARY

October 10

l to r Eleanor Roosevelt (Trustee), Mary Winslow (Office of the Coordinator of Inter-American Affairs), Senorita Maria Josephina Albano (Honorary Degree Recipient). Used with permission of the Archives of The Sage Colleges.

TWENTY-FIFTH ANNIVERSARY

October 10

l to r front row Concha Romero James (Honorary Degree Recipient), Marina Nunez del Prado (Honorary Degree Recipient), Graciela Mandujano (Honorary Degree Recipient), James L. Meader (President, RSC), Eleanor Roosevelt (Trustee), Ester Neira de Calvo (Honorary Degree Recipient), Ana Rosa de Martinez Guerrero (Honorary Degree Recipient); *second row* unidentified man. *The Times Record* October 11, 1941. Used with permission of *The Troy Record* Troy, New York.

TWENTY-FIFTH ANNIVERSARY STAGE PARTY

October 10

Seated *l to r* Unidentified Clergyman, Dr. Luis Quintianilla (Minister Plenipotentiary of Mexico), Eleanor Roosevelt (Trustee), James Meader (President, RSC), Mr. Thomas Burke (Chief, Division of International Communications, U.S. Department of State), Dr. Vincente Valdés Rodriquez (Counselor of the Cuban Embassy). Used with permission of the Archives of The Sage Colleges.

BESTOWING OF HONORARY DEGREE

October 10

l to r Dr. James Meader (President, RSC), Senorita Marina Núñez del Prado (Bolivia), Dr. V. Valdés Rodriquez (Counselor, Cuban Embassy), Eleanor Roosevelt (Trustee). Used with permission of the Archives of The Sage Colleges.

TWENTY-FIFTH ANNIVERSARY

Donkey Cart. Used with permission of the Archives of The Sage Colleges.

TWENTY-FIFTH ANNIVERSARY

l to r Peggy Ann Carlisle, Marguerite Coursen, Margaret Straub, help prepare the street for repaving and renaming in honor of Simon Bolivar in preparation for a street fiesta. Used with permission of the Archives of The Sage Colleges.

Danza De Huaka-Tokoris-1936 Sculpture by M. Núñez del Prado exhibited during the Twenty-fifth Anniversary Celebration. Used with permission of the Archives of The Sage Colleges.

CULMINATING FIESTA OF
THE TWENTY-FIFTH ANNIVERSARY

Sage Park

Julian Huarte and the Tropicana Orchestra (music), Lao and Monista (Dancers from Cuba), dancing the Huaka-Tokoris Dance before the public dancing began. Used with permission of the Archives of The Sage Colleges.

1944 COMMENCEMENT

l to r George D. Stoddard (President, New York State Board of Education), Katharine Burr Blodgett (Honorary Degree Recipient), Sophie Van S. Theis (Honorary Degree Recipient), Margaret Webster (Honorary Degree Recipient) and Helen McKinstry (President, RSC). Original photograph courtesy of Gunn, used with permission of the Archives of The Sage Colleges.

1945 COMMENCEMENT

l to r Unnamed faculty member, Dorothy C. Stratton (Honorary Degree Recipient) and unnamed trustee. Used with permission of the Archives of The Sage Colleges.

1947 COMMENCEMENT

l to r Alice Morgan Wright (Honorary Degree Recipient), Helen McKinstry (President, RSC), Ruth Fulton Benedict (Honorary Degree Recipient), Florence Ellinwood Allen (Honorary Degree Recipient), Emily Hickman (Honorary Degree Recipient). Used with permission of the Archives of The Sage Colleges.

1952 COMMENCEMENT

l to r Lewis Froman (President, RSC), Elizabeth Gray Vining (Honorary Degree Recipient), Patsy Pai (RSC Class of 1952). Translation of the Chinese characters; *Under the sky all men are one family.* Original photograph is by Gene Baxter of Troy, used with permission of the Archives of The Sage Colleges.

1954 COMMENCEMENT- GUESTS

l to r Arnold Branch (husband of Doris Emrick Lee), Doris Emrick Lee (Honorary Degree Recipient), Lewis Froman (President, RSC), Mrs. Oswald B. Lord, Mrs. and Mr. John A. Becker of Castleton. Used with permission of the Archives of The Sage Colleges.

1955 COMMENCEMENT

l to r Lewis Froman (President, RSC) and Jacqueline Cochran (Honorary Degree Recipient). Used with permission of the Archives of The Sage Colleges.

1972 COMMENCEMENT

l to r Stephen H. Sampson (Honorary Degree Recipient), Marina von Neumann Whitman (Honorary Degree Recipient), Dorothy L. Brown (Honorary Degree Recipient), Charles U. Walker (President, RSC). Used with permission of the Archives of The Sage Colleges.

1973 COMMENCEMENT

l to r Dr. Virginia Apgar (Honorary Degree Recipient), Dr. Grace Jorgensen, Dr. Collins (Trustee). Used with permission of the Archives of The Sage Colleges.

l to r Tenley Albright (1975 Honorary Degree Recipient) and Mary Kosloski (1955 March of Dimes Poster Child and RSC faculty member from 1978- ~1986). Personal Collection of Mary Kosloski Garrett, used with her permission.

1983 COMMENCEMENT

l to r Thomas Sweeney (Faculty Member), Grace Murray Hopper (Honorary Degree Recipient), and William F. Kahl (President, RSC). Personal Collection of Tom Sweeney, used with his permission.

1990 COMMENCEMENT

l to r Sara Chapman (President, RSC), Gertrude B. Elion (Honorary Degree Recipient), unknown trustee. Used with permission of the Archives of The Sage Colleges.

1992 COMMENCEMENT

Ann Caracristi (Honorary Degree Recipient). Used with permission of the Archives of The Sage Colleges.

.

Maria Goeppert-Mayer, Ph.D.

DOCTOR OF SCIENCE-1960

Theoretical Physicist, Author, Educator, Nobel Laureate in Physics

Maria Goeppert-Mayer (1906-1972) was born in Kattowitz, Upper Silesia, Germany into a tradition of scientific and academic exploration. On her paternal side, she was destined to be the seventh continuous generation of university professors. In 1924 she began university education at the University of Goettingen. Although her original aspiration was to be a mathematician, she switched to physics early in her academic career. In 1930 she earned her Ph.D. in Theoretical Physics. Her doctoral committee undoubtedly set a high bar with two Nobel laureates (James Franck- Physics, 1925 and Adolf Windhaus- Chemistry, 1928) and one future Nobel Prize winner (Max Born- Physics, 1954) on her committee.

Goeppert's father died while she was at the University and her mother took in student boarders so they could remain in their home. Joseph Mayer, an American physical chemist and Rockefeller Fellow, was one of their boarders. Goeppert and Mayer married in early 1930 and shortly after finishing her doctorate, the couple moved to Baltimore, Maryland where he had a position at Johns Hopkins. Despite her credentials and scientific genealogy, Dr. Goeppert-Mayer was unable to find a paid position as a research scientist since it was the Depression and she was female. Many institutions had nepotism rules that prevented spouses from being hired so in essence, that meant only the male of the pair got a job. The Depression made women even less likely to be hired. Goeppert-Mayer was frequently and eagerly offered volunteer positions with teaching, research, mentoring, and administrative duties. These were equivalent to faculty positions, but without the pay. In fact, it took twenty-nine years after she earned her doctorate before she was able to get a full-time, paid position in her field.

Fortunately, Dr. Goeppert-Mayer was able to find scientifically rewarding work as a volunteer or consultant in various laboratories during those years. At Johns Hopkins, she was able to work with Karl F. Herzfeld and expanded her knowledge of Chemical Physics and earned a reputation as a demanding teacher. When her husband accepted a job at Columbia University, she accepted a part-time position teaching undergraduates at Sarah Lawrence. She also worked as a volunteer in the laboratory of Harold Urey, a 1934 Nobel laureate for his discovery of the heavy isotope of hydrogen. In charge of the Substitute Alloy Materials research group of the Manhattan Project, Urey assigned Goeppert-Mayer to work on the possibility of separating isotopes by a photochemical reaction. Goeppert-Mayer's work, however, did not result in a method for isotope separation. While at Columbia, she also worked on a project calculating expected energy levels of transuranic and rare earth isotopes, unstable elements that radioactively decay. When Enrico Fermi, another physicist in the department, assumed greater responsibility with the Manhattan Project, Goeppert-Mayer took over his teaching responsibilities with only twenty-four hours notice.

After the war, Drs. Mayer and Goeppert-Mayer and their two children moved to Chicago. Both were offered positions at the University of Chicago, but hers was as a voluntary associate professor. Fortunately, a former student of Goeppert-Mayer offered her a half-time position as a Research Physicist at the nearby Argonne National Laboratories. There Goeppert-Mayer acquired knowledge in another area of physics, Nuclear Physics. In time, she applied this new knowledge to a problem that she and Edward Teller had been exploring on the origin of the elements. Using data for isotopic abundance, Goeppert-Mayer noticed a series of "magic numbers" that led to unusual stability when the nuclei had 2, 8, 20, 50, or 82 neutrons or protons or 126 neutrons. In a discussion of the problem with Fermi, in which he asked if there was any chance of spin-orbit coupling, she recognized that spin-orbit coupling was the key to the solution. She published a model of the nuclear spin-orbit interaction that explained many experimental observations in a simple way. Independently and almost simultaneously, a group at the University of Heidelberg led by the theorist J. Hans D. Jensen proposed the same model.

In 1959 Drs. Mayer and Goeppert-Mayer were offered full professorships at the University of California, San Diego in a new graduate program. Both were paid positions. The University of Chicago countered with an offer to pay Dr. Goeppert-Mayer as a full-time full professor, fourteen years *after* she started working for them on a voluntary basis. She declined, and in September 1960 they moved to California.

On May 29, 1960 the degree of Doctor of Science was conferred on Dr.

Goeppert-Mayer by Russell Sage College, in recognition of her monumental contributions to the theory of nuclear shell structure and her seminal work *Statistical Mechanics*, coauthored with her husband, Dr. Joseph Mayer.

In October 1960 Goeppert-Mayer suffered a stroke and never fully regained her health, although she continued to work and travel. Much of her professional energy went into her teaching after her stroke.

In 1963 Goeppert-Mayer, Jensen, and Eugene Wigner shared the Nobel Prize in Physics. In her biographical information supplied by the Official Web Site of The Nobel Prize, her Honorary Degree of Doctor of Science from Russel [sic] Sage College is cited. Allegedly, a San Diego newspaper had the headline "S.D. Mother Wins Nobel Prize."

In addition to the Nobel Prize, Dr. Goeppert-Mayer was elected a member of the National Academy of Sciences, the American Philosophical Society, a fellow of the American Physical Society, and a fellow of the American Academy of Arts and Sciences. At the time of her election to the National Academy of Sciences, only six women had been elected in the one hundred year existence of the Academy. Dr. Maria Goeppert-Mayer died in La Jolla, California on February 20, 1972.

Dorothy L. Brown, M.D.

DOCTOR OF SCIENCE-1972

First African-American Woman Surgeon in the South,
First African-American Woman Tennessee Legislator

The early years of Dorothy L. Brown (1919-2004) gave little indication of the trail of firsts that she would blaze. She was born in Philadelphia, Pennsylvania to a mother who recognized by the time that her daughter was five months old, that she could not care for her. She placed her daughter in Vanderheyden Hall orphanage in Troy, New York located across the street from the Emma Willard School, a boarding school for predominantly wealthy, white girls. Her first thirteen years in many ways highlighted the differences between her dreams and her reality. On one side of the street, were white girls of privilege afforded wonderful educational and social opportunities. On the other side, were girls, mostly white, who were orphaned and whose opportunities and ambitions were more limited. Then there were the few non-white children, like Brown, whose opportunities were also limited by race. The few times that the worlds mixed, when the orphans were invited to Emma Willard, the non-white girls (3 of 250 residents) were left behind. Seeing and hearing about what was available to the girls at Emma Willard fanned a drive in Brown to succeed.

At the age of five Brown underwent a tonsillectomy, and the procedure sparked an interest in medicine for her. She was possessed of determination and rare self-knowledge for her young age. Noticing that she was one of the few children who never had a visitor, Brown went to the Superintendent of the Orphanage, Mr. Herbert Hunn, and told him that she wanted visitors. Mr. Hunn arranged for a local family, the Coffeens, to visit her; a relationship developed and the Coffeens became one of many people in the community who helped and encouraged the young African-American girl to achieve her dreams. In fact, Janet Coffeen Craw, RSC '32, and Brown kept in touch by mail throughout their lives.

Shortly before Brown's thirteenth birthday, her mother reappeared in her life. The two did not get along and Brown kept running back to the orphanage. Her mother finally placed her in service as a mother's helper with the Jarretts, an Albany family. According to Brown, she discussed with the Jarretts her desire to become an M.D. The Jarretts had a large home library that they encouraged her to use. Brown saved her money and when she was fifteen, the Jarretts agreed that she could return to Troy to attend high school. With their help and that of Mr. Hunn, Brown was placed as a foster child in the home of Mr. and Mrs. Redmon and she enrolled in Troy High School.

The Redmons considered her to be their daughter and encouraged her to adopt their Christian values and outlook. Later in life, Brown expressed gratitude for the influence the Redmons had on her. She attributed their influence to showing her how to forgive oppression without bitterness or loss of dignity.

Graduating at the top of her class from Troy High School and wanting to attend college, the Troy Methodist Women nominated Brown for a scholarship to Bennett College in Greensboro, North Carolina. She was awarded the scholarship and combined with the money she had saved, she was able to enroll in Bennett in 1937. After her first year, Bennett College administrators suggested to the Troy Methodist Women, that Brown was not Bennett material and that she should not return for a second year. No one told Brown, and she returned and graduated in 1941, second in her class. Although she was encouraged to prepare for a career as a teacher, Dorothy managed to take all of the courses necessary to attend medical school.

After graduation from Bennett, she returned to Troy to find work so that she could pay for medical school. With her college degree in hand, the only job she could get was as a presser in a large commercial laundry. Once the U.S. entered WWII, she was able to get a job as a civilian inspector of army ordnance. She was met with much resistance and discrimination as one of only a handful of African-American women defense workers in upstate New York.

By 1944 she had saved quite a bit of money and had been accepted at both Howard and Meharry Medical Schools. Brown chose Meharry because the cost of living was lower in Tennessee than in Washington, D.C. Once again the Troy Methodist Women as well as Herbert Hunn came to her aid, helping her meet the cost of medical school.

After completing medical school, Brown was unable to find a surgical residency program that would accept her. This time the discrimination was gender-based as male surgeons thought that the rigors of surgery were too much for females. She returned to Meharry and talked the Chief of Surgery, Dr. Matthew Walker, into accepting her into his program over the objections of his staff. Brown worked so hard to prove herself she was nicknamed "Mule." When she completed her surgical residency in 1954, she became the first African-American woman surgeon in the south. She also was one of a very few African-Americans elected a Fellow in the American College of Surgeons.

Outside of the surgical field, Dr. Brown also broke new ground. In 1956 she became the first single woman in Tennessee to adopt a child. When her daughter, Lola, reached high school age, Brown enrolled her in the Emma Willard School in Troy. Brown was also elected to the Tennessee state legislature, becoming the first African-American woman to serve in that body.

On May 21, 1972 the degree of Doctor of Science was conferred on Dr. Brown by Russell Sage College, in honor of her "determination, hard work, professional success, and for (her) warm and human manner. Clearly in (her) career (she) met and quietly but thoroughly overcame momentous obstacles and difficulties."[45]

Dr. Brown's determination and unrelenting drive to become a surgeon—despite the obstacles she encountered as a poor, African-American female with no family— kept her active in her profession through the early 1990s. She began work on an autobiography, with the working title *Mule* but died in 2004 at 85, before completing her book.

---

[45] Ibid.

Virginia Apgar, M.D., M.P.H.

DOCTOR OF HUMANE LETTERS-1973

Medical Pioneer in Anesthesiology, Neonatology, and Teratology

Virginia Apgar (1909-1974) was a pioneer in three fields; anesthesiology, neonatology, and teratology. Her name is recognized worldwide because she developed the neonatal scoring system known as the Apgar score. The five assessments done at one and five minutes post-birth match the letters in Apgar's name: **A**ctivity; **P**ulse; **G**rimace; **A**ppearance; **R**espiration.

Dr. Apgar earned her A.B. in Zoology from Mount Holyoke (1929) and an M.D. from Columbia University College of Physicians and Surgeons (P&S) (1933). She did a surgical residency at P & S from 1933-35. Dr. Apgar was encouraged to shift to anesthesiology by a mentor who suggested that the prospects for a female surgeon during the Depression were dismal but anesthesiology was not yet a well-recognized specialty. After completing a training course in anesthesiology for nurses, and six-month residencies in anesthesiology in Wisconsin and New York City, Dr. Apgar was appointed Clinical Director of the Division of Anesthesiology at Presbyterian Hospital and attending anesthetist in 1938. She was the first woman to head a division at Presbyterian.

Her title of Clinical Director, however, was somewhat misleading. Many surgeons did not accept anesthesiologists as equals, so the pay was low and Dr. Apgar had a difficult time recruiting physicians to work with her. In fact, she was the only staff member until the mid-1940s. At that time, anesthesia was acknowledged as a medical specialty with required residency training. In 1949 anesthesiology became a full academic department. Although Dr. Apgar expected to be appointed as the first Chair of the department, a male colleague was appointed instead. Dr. Apgar was, however, appointed Full Professor of Anesthesiology at P & S, the first such appointment and the first female Full Professor at P & S. Involuntarily freed from administrative duties, Dr. Apgar had more time for research.

Concerned about the effect of maternal anesthesia on neonates, she devised and tested the scoring method eventually known as the Apgar score. The plan was to use it as a screening method to evaluate newborn health with an eye to appropriate resuscitation protocols to reduce mortality. The method was published in 1953.

As Apgar and others began looking at the various factors that might impact Apgar scores, Apgar began to note instances of birth defects. By the late fifties, Dr. Apgar had attended over 17,000 births. To acquire the statistical skills she needed to correlate her findings and those of others, she took a sabbatical to enroll at the Johns Hopkins School of Public Health. After earning her M.P.H. (1959) she joined the National Foundation- March of Dimes (NF) as head of the new Division of Congenital Malformations. Eventually, Dr. Apgar became the Vice-President for Medical Affairs for NF.

At NF, Dr. Apgar continued her research into the causes of birth defects and continued in her role as educator by informing others of her findings. She was the first person to hold an academic appointment (as Clinical Professor of Pediatrics) at Cornell University School of Medicine in this emerging area of teratology (the study of birth defects). She was also a lecturer in medical genetics at Johns Hopkins School of Public Health. Her students respected her knowledge and her ability to impart enormous amounts of information in a very rapid way.

On May 20, 1973 the degree of Doctor of Humane Letters was conferred on Dr. Apgar by Russell Sage College, in recognition of her "contributions as a scientist, physician, educator and public servant, and because of [her] a warm and human manner ..."[46]

Virginia Apgar never formally retired, remaining professionally active until shortly before her death. She also continued with her self-described leisure activities throughout her life: she was an accomplished violinist, playing with chamber quartets and building stringed instruments; a gardener; a fly fisherman; a golfer; a stamp collector; and a pilot. She chose to confront discrimination by establishing new fields in which she could and did excel. She remained curious about all she encountered throughout her life, thereby avoiding becoming rigid or hidebound in her thoughts or actions. Dr. Apgar died in August 1974 at the age of 65.

Twenty years after her death, a postage stamp bearing her likeness was issued by the U.S. Postal Service as part of their Great Americans Series, an appropriate

---

[46] Ibid.

tribute for a dedicated stamp collector like Apgar. It was also an appropriate tribute that the stamp was released during the annual meeting of the American Academy of Pediatrics, since Dr. L. Joseph Butterfield, Professor of Pediatrics at the University of Colorado was the chairman of the committee that worked for many years to get a stamp issued in Virginia Apgar's honor.

Tenley E. Albright, M.D.

DOCTOR OF SCIENCE-1975

Olympic Gold Medalist, Surgeon, Scholar

Tenley Albright was born in Newton Centre, Massachusetts on July 18, 1935. Her father, Hollis, was a surgeon in Boston and her mother, Elin, an artist. When Tenley received her first pair of skates for Christmas, the hockey skates were quickly exchanged for figure skates. Her age when she got those first skates was variously reported as six, eight, and nine. Initially, she skated in her flooded backyard with other neighborhood children.

She did not do significant amounts of skating in her early years. Her father, a surgeon in the Army, was posted to El Paso, Texas and then to Grass Valley, California, neither post having outdoor ice available. When her father was sent overseas to be Chief of Surgery at the Ninety-third General Hospital in Wales, Tenley, her younger brother Niles, and their mother returned to Boston.

After seeing an amateur ice show at the famous Skating Club of Boston (SCOB), Tenley told her mother that she wanted to learn figure skating. Due to wartime gas rationing, she was only able to take lessons once a month, eventually increasing to once a week. She took lessons from Willie Frick and Maribel Vinson, prominent teachers at SCOB.

In 1946 shortly before her eleventh birthday, Tenley noticed the first symptoms of polio while holding her infant cousin. Her neck, back, and legs were affected, She was put in isolation in an infectious disease hospital (Haynes Memorial in Allston, Massachusetts) with a polio sign on the door. In those pre-Salk vaccine days, polio was a frightening disease. The means of transmission was unclear as was the causative agent. The outcomes were also uncertain. Some patients were permanently paralyzed, some even forced to live in an iron lung. Others recovered with no permanent paralysis. The only treatment was packing the affected areas with steamed, hot towels, a treatment known as "Sister Kenny Treatments" after the pioneering nurse.

Tenley was one of the fortunate ones. She remembers a doctor coming in to see her on a Monday after she had been bedridden for months. He told her that he expected to come back on Friday and see her take three steps. Tenley spent the intervening days imagining walking those three steps. Friday came, she walked the three steps, and her recovery began.[47] Albright always remembered her time in the hospital and those things that eased a very scary time, like having someone hold her hand during her first lumbar puncture. She used what she learned as a patient to make experiences easier for her patients.

When Albright was finally released from the hospital, she was very weak. Her legs could barely support her body. The doctors urged her to continue to exercise to strengthen her muscles, but also warned her parents that due to the fear of polio and the lack of knowledge about how it was spread, Albright would not be welcome at venues in which people would be gathered. As a way to strengthen her muscles in a venue that was fairly solitary, her parents allowed her to go back to skating, an activity she had enjoyed before her illness. The first time back on skates, she had to hold on to the wall and inch along hand over hand as she moved on the ice.

Albright worked hard at recovering her strength and within months, she had won her first skating title, New England Juvenile Champion. Her recovery from polio complete, Albright went on to win five National Championships each year from 1952-1956; the North American Championship in 1953 and 1955; an Olympic Silver Medal in figure skating in 1952 in Oslo, Norway; and a Gold Medal in figure skating in 1956 in Cortina, Italy. In two years, 1953 and 1955, she won the top three championships; United States, North American, and World. She was the first U.S. woman to win an Olympic Gold Medal in figure skating.

The Gold Medal in Cortina was especially gratifying. Albright had sliced her right ankle to the bone during practice two weeks before the competition. Her father flew to Italy and repaired her ankle. During her free skate, set to the music of *Tales of Hoffman,* the *Bacharole*, the largely European crowd hummed along with the music. She remembers: "That actually lifted me up."[48] Albright also won both the New England and Eastern Pairs Championships in 1951 with Dudley Richards. Albright suffered a concussion in practice with Richards, so

---

[47] Academy of Achievement, "Tenley Albright-Interview," Accessed August 18, 2015, http://www.achievement.org/autodoc/page/albOint-1.

[48] Tenley Albright, "Is your name Tenley, too?" Accessed September 18, 2015, http//mynameistenley.com/about-tenley-albright/.

she went back to singles skating after the Championships.

While Albright was competing in skating, she was also a student at Radcliffe, going to summer school in order to graduate with her class. Although not majoring in a science, she completed all of the required pre-med classes in order to pursue her other dream, becoming a medical doctor. In 1957 she entered Harvard Medical School with the intent of becoming a pediatrician, without finishing her undergraduate degree. Since Albright returned to school without becoming a professional skater, she is still listed as an amateur skater. When asked if skating had helped her in her later medical career, Albright said that among the things she learned from skating were to get up after you fall and to continue to learn new things.

When Albright entered Harvard Medical School, she was one of five women in a class of about 140 students. She admitted that initially it was an adjustment on many levels, but she persevered and graduated. When she began medical school, Albright had planned to go into pediatrics, but during the course of her training she switched her specialty to surgery.

In response to a question about the need to concentrate intently in both surgery and competitive skating, Albright's lengthy response gives important insight into her character as it relates to training both as a competitive skater and as a surgeon.

"There is a very interesting balance, because sometimes when we are intensely concentrating, we also need to have our other antenna up. Maybe we are talking about training ourselves to focus on what we need to. Sometimes that seems as if we are blocking out other things, but there is still an awareness of them. I don't know how really to explain that. But certainly you do that in taking off on a double axel. You have to concentrate on what you are doing, but obviously, if somebody is coming down the ice about to bump into you, you've got to be aware of that. But not so much that you don't think of exactly what you are doing, or you will fall flat on the jump itself."

"In surgery, you have to think of exactly what you are doing when the scalpel is in your hand, and your focus is exactly on what it is you are doing. If you aren't concentrating, and you are not placing that tiny, tiny incision in just the proper point in the common duct, you could be in real trouble, and the patient too. And you can't allow yourself not to concentrate. But you also have to be aware, so that if something is happening in any other part of the operating field, you sense that too, because you mustn't ignore that while you are concentrating on this thing. It's a very, very interesting balance of concentrating and awareness. And our minds are capable of phenomenal things. Perhaps that's something we should study more and find out more about. Most great people – athletes, scientists, Nobel Prize winners, movie producers – know that they've had to concentrate but allow their minds to think in many areas at once. If they didn't, while they were working to solve something, they wouldn't be able to think of alternative solutions. It's exciting."[49]

After completing medical school Albright trained as a surgeon, eventually going into practice in Boston with her father and brother Niles. Not surprisingly, her practice included sports injuries. She also married and had three daughters.

On May 25, 1975 the degree of Doctor of Science was conferred on Tenley Albright by Russell Sage College, in part to recognize her continued successes in multiple arenas, often thought to be exclusive, at least for women. Her citation in part notes that Albright has "… shown that the roles of athlete, scholar, surgeon, wife and mother are within the reach of one woman."[50]

After 23 years in practice as a surgeon on-call every other night and every other weekend, Albright switched her attention to health advocacy and research. In 2005 she founded the MIT (Massachusetts Institute of Technology) Collaborative Institute. This initiative encourages addressing systemic, entrenched societal issues through interaction and engagement of experts from a broad range of fields, both those involved from traditional disciplines and those from without.

Albright continues to be active in organizations important to her. In 1980, she became the first woman officer of the U.S. Olympic Committee, helping to develop an Athletes' Advisory Committee. She has remained active with the March of Dimes and Harvard Medical School. She has served multiple roles with the National Library of Medicine and the National Institutes of Health. Albright's list of awards and involvements is lengthy and diverse.

---

[49] Tenley Albright. Academy of Achievement. "Tenley Albright-Interview." Accessed August 18, 2015. http://www.achievement.org/autodoc/page/albOint-1
[50] Honorary Degree Collection, Archives, The Sage Colleges.

Her Honorary Degree from Russell Sage College is one of eight she received (as of 2011). In October 2015 Dr. Albright was inducted into the National Women's Hall of Fame in Seneca Falls, New York. Dr. Albright lives in the greater Boston area and continues to be interested in the intersection of many fields and how they can be used to solve problems. She certainly fulfills James Meader's criterion that an Honorary Degree recipient continue to make societal contributions after being awarded an honorary degree from RSC.

Grace Murray Hopper, Ph.D.

DOCTOR OF SCIENCE-1983

First Female Programmer of the Harvard Mark I, Head of the Team that Developed COBOL, Officer with the Longest Active Duty Service in the U.S.N.

Grace Brewster Murray (1906-1992) received her basic education at private schools for girls and women, earning a B.A. in Mathematics and Physics from Vassar College in 1928. From there she went to Yale University and earned an M.A. in Mathematics and Physics (1930) and a Ph.D. in Mathematics (1934) becoming the first woman to earn a Ph.D. in Mathematics from Yale. Her first job was as a Mathematics Instructor at Vassar (1931-1945) and during this time, she also married Vincent Foster Hopper. They divorced in 1945 with no children and he was later killed in WWII.

After Pearl Harbor Grace Murray Hopper, as she was now known, tried to enlist in the United States Navy. She was turned down because of her advanced age of 35, and her weight/height ratio of 105 pounds to 5'6" and because the Navy thought her mathematics skills would be more valuable in a civilian role. Undaunted, Hopper joined the Navy WAVES (Woman Accepted for Voluntary Emergency Service) in December 1943. After graduation from the Midshipman's School for Women at Mount Holyoke, she was assigned to the Bureau of Ordnance's Computation Project at Harvard University as a Lieutenant (Junior Grade). There she worked on the world's first large-scale computer, the Harvard Mark I. During this tour of duty, Lt. Hopper became the first female programmer. Released from active duty in 1946, Hopper maintained her connection with the Navy as a reservist.

She resigned from Vassar and became a Research Fellow in Engineering Sciences and Applied Physics in the Harvard Computation Laboratory. Subsequently she joined the Eckert-Mauchley Computer Corporation, forerunner of Sperry Rand, where she was involved in the development of the first commercial electronic computer, the UNIVAC (**Uni**versal **A**utomatic **C**omputer). Programming had to be done using binary code, the only language understood by the computer, so in 1952 Hopper developed the first compiler, a routine to convert instructions into machine code. This laid the foundation for compilers to convert high-level language into machine language.

During the mid-50s Hopper developed a compiler for UNIVAC, called FLOW-MATIC, which converted English words, such as "Write" and "Input," into machine code. Her initial efforts substituted French for English words, an effort squashed by her bosses. From 1959-61 Hopper headed a team that developed a language eventually known as COBOL (**Co**mmon-**B**usiness-**O**riented-**L**anguage) allowing computers to respond to words rather than numbers.

Remaining active in the naval reserves during her civilian career, Commander Grace Murray Hopper retired from the USNR at the end of 1966. She was recalled to active duty in 1967 for a six-month assignment, which was changed to an indefinite tour of duty that lasted almost twenty years, until 1986.

In March 1983 Morley Safer of *60 Minutes* interviewed the then 76-year-old Captain Hopper. When Congressman Phillip Crane (D-IL) saw the interview, he introduced a bill to promote her to the rank of Commodore by special Presidential appointment. Her appearance on television brought her to the attention of people who had not known of her work. Commodore Hopper began receiving multiple requests to speak and accept Honorary Degrees but she turned them down. Fortunately, she had accepted the invitation from Russell Sage College prior to the Safer interview.

On May 22, 1983 the degree of Doctor of Science was conferred on Commodore Hopper by Russell Sage College. It was in recognition of her pioneering work in computers as well as for the fact that she was an officer with the longest active duty service in the United States Navy.

In 1985 she was named a Rear Admiral and when she involuntarily retired on August 14, 1986, she was the oldest active duty officer in the US Navy. In the mid-1990s, the Navy named an Aegis Destroyer "Hopper" in honor of Admiral Hopper. Also in the mid-1990s, The Sage Colleges named their first computer network "hopper" after Admiral Hopper.

Dr. Hopper died in her sleep in Arlington, Virginia. on January 1, 1992. She was buried with full military honors at Arlington National Cemetery.

Gertrude Elion, M.S.

DOCTOR OF SCIENCE-1990

Researcher, Educator, Nobel Laureate in Physiology or Medicine

Gertrude Elion (1918-1999) was a prodigious scientific talent. Graduating from Hunter College in 1937, Ms. Elion began a seven-year search for a job that utilized her abilities. A woman chemist during the Depression was not considered an ideal employee. Initially she got a temporary job teaching biochemistry to nurses enrolled in the New York Hospital School of Nursing, and at the end of the three-month trimester, she got a volunteer job as a laboratory assistant. After a year and half in this position (eventually she was paid twenty dollars per week), she enrolled in a master's program in Chemistry at New York University (NYU). She completed her course work in a year. After taking a job as a substitute teacher in chemistry, physics and general science, she did the required research work for her M.S. at NYU on weekends and at night. In 1941 she earned her M.S. in Chemistry.

As WWII progressed, jobs became more available for women as the numbers of civilian men dropped, and Elion got a job doing analytical quality control at the Quaker Maid Company. This was an opportunity to learn instrumentation techniques, but the work itself was very repetitive and unchallenging. Looking for something more interesting and challenging, she worked for a short time at a laboratory at Johnson and Johnson until the lab disbanded. She was next hired as a laboratory assistant to Dr. George H. Hitchings at Burroughs-Wellcome. This productive affiliation continued for forty years.

The relationship between Dr. Hitchings and Ms. Elion was unusual in many ways. Recognizing Elion's enormous talent and drive for knowledge, Hitchings encouraged Elion to expand her knowledge and responsibility. In her Nobel Prize autobiography, Elion noted that when she started working with Hitchings, she was solely an organic chemist. As she became involved in the biological activities of the compounds she was synthesizing and the microbiology of the test systems, Hitchings encouraged her to expand her horizons into biochemistry, pharmacology, immunology, and virology. Their collaboration became a very productive scientific partnership.

During her early years with Hitchings, Elion worked in Tuckahoe, Westchester County, New York and commuted evenings to Brooklyn Polytechnic Institute, as she worked part-time toward her doctorate. After several years, the school informed her that she had to be full-time to complete her doctorate. Elion admitted that making the decision to retain her job instead of completing her doctorate was difficult, but she had found a challenging, rewarding job, and she needed to support herself. Hitchings reinforced her decision and told her that she wouldn't be held back because of a lack of a doctorate. Years later after she had received multiple honorary doctorates, she decided that it had been the right decision.

When Elion and Hitchings began their collaboration, little was known about the metabolism of nucleic acids. Their studies began before Watson and Crick published their paper about the structure of DNA. Elion and Hitchings decided to take an approach in which they would study the synthesis of nucleic acids in normal cells and compare their findings to observations in malignant cells, or those infected with pathogens. They thought that this approach might suggest points at which compounds could be developed that selectively blocked a nucleic acid pathway used by a malignant cell, or a pathogen, without blocking the normal pathway. Doing careful, painstaking laboratory work, this approach led to the synthesis of a number of very important compounds including: 6-mercaptopurine, the first purine antagonist to treat acute lymphoblastic leukemia in children; acycloguanosine, an antiviral drug used to treat *Herpes simplex* (causes cold sores), *Varicella zoster* (causes chicken pox), and *Herpes zoster* (causes shingles); azathioprine, used to help prevent organ transplant rejections and to treat severe rheumatoid arthritis (an autoimmune disease); allopurinol, used to treat gout, Chagas' disease and Leshmaniasis disease; and pyrimethamine, an antiparasistic compound used to treat malaria and being investigated as a potential treatment for amyotrophic lateral sclerosis (ALS or Lou Gehrig's Disease), and late onset Tay-Sachs disease.

In 1988 the Nobel Committee recognized the foundational approach that Elion and Hitchings took by awarding them the Nobel Prize in Physiology or Medicine. They shared the prize with Sir James Black of the United Kingdom. Elion was one of a small number of women who won the Nobel Prize in one of the scientific fields and one of an even smaller number of Nobel winners in a scientific field without an earned doctorate.

Elion retired from the Research Triangle Park facility of Burroughs-Wellcome (now known as Glaxo Wellcome) in 1983. She remained active as *Scientist Emerita* until her death in 1999, publishing her last paper in 1998. She published many scientific papers, was the holder of 45 patents, 23 Honorary Degrees, was a member of the National Academy of Science, was the first woman elected to the National Inventors Hall of Fame, and had a long list of other honors.

On May 20, 1990 the degree of Doctor of Science was conferred on Gertrude Elion by Russell Sage College, in recognition that "she was an exemplary scientist, a caring mentor of young scientists and a model of contributive humanitarianism."[51]

One role in which Elion excelled was that of teacher and mentor. Even in retirement, she continued to mentor a third-year medical student who took a year-long leave from classes and learned how to do research by working in the laboratory with her. She also mentored graduate students and took them into her laboratory.

In his book, *The Greatest Generation,* Tom Brokaw, quotes Dr. Thomas Krenitsky, founder of Krenitsky Pharmaceuticals and a former student of Elion's, "Trudy [Gertrude Elion] was a role model for women but she was a role model for men too."[52]

In 1992 the Chemistry Department of Russell Sage College offered a Special Topics Course in which the students selected an area of Elion's research, read all of her published papers on that topic and presented the work to the rest of the class. The culminating activity of the class was the opportunity to discuss the work with Elion. Elion spent two days with the students, answering any and all questions they had, ranging from why she had done a particular experiment, what she had tried that had not worked out, to the role of women in industrial research and its rewards and barriers. It was an incredible experience for all involved.

Elion collapsed while on her daily walk on February 21, 1999 and she died later that day at the University of North Carolina Hospital.

---

[51] Ibid.

[52] Thomas Krenitsky quoted in Tom Brokaw, *The Greatest Generation* (New York: Random House, 1998) 306.

Ann Caracristi, B.A.

DOCTOR OF PUBLIC SERVICE-1992

Cryptologist, Deputy Director of the NSA, RSC Graduate

Ann Caracristi (1921-) earned her B.A. in English and History from Russell Sage College in 1942 while the world was at war on multiple fronts. Dr. Meader, President of RSC and the administrators had been working hard preparing the students and the college to contribute to the war effort. Doris L. Crockett, a legendary and well-loved administrator, urged Ms. Caracristi to do her part for the war effort and join the Army Signal Intelligence Service (ASIS). ASIS had contacted RSC in their campaign for recruits.

Assigned to the cryptology group, Caracristi worked to decode Japanese transmissions during WWII for the ASIS from 1942-45. After working as a civilian journalist for a year, she decided to go back to cryptology. From 1946-52, she worked as a research analyst for the Army Security Agency and the Armed Forces Security Agency. There she applied her cryptology expertise to decoding Soviet intelligence transmissions during the Cold War and in 1952, she became the Chief of Operations Elements in the newly formed National Security Agency (NSA). Much of the specific work done by Caracristi remains classified.

We do know that she was promoted within the agency several times and was appointed the Deputy Director of the NSA in April 1980. She served as the sixth Deputy Director until her retirement from NSA in 1982. Caracristi received many awards for her service, including the Federal Woman's Award (1965), the NSA Meritorious Civilian Service Award (1966), the NSA Exceptional Civilian Service Award (1975), the Career Service Award, National Civil Service League (1978), and the Department of Defense Distinguished Civilian Service Award (1980). The citation from the Department of Defense recognized Caracristi for thirty-seven years of outstanding service in cryptology. The citation stated that Caracristi "has been in the forefront of cryptologic development, as a gifted cryptologist, a valued advisor, and an innovative manager. She is personally responsible for many of the major decisions affecting cryptologic production techniques, and she has helped to shape national cryptologic policies. Miss Caracristi's exceptional contributions to the nation's security warrant the highest recognition this department can bestow."[53]

On May 17, 1992 the Doctor of Public Service degree was conferred on Ann Caracristi by Russell Sage College, in recognition of her leadership in matters of national security, especially the leadership shown in using "relationships among various fields of study and understanding the emerging power of developing technologies . . .[and to see] connections among mathematics, technology, linguistics and humane studies."[54] This ability to see the connections was not always apparent or valued.

After her retirement from the NSA, Caracristi remained active in the intelligence community, serving on a number of Presidential and NSA advisory boards. She served as President (1989-91) of the Association of Former Intelligence Officers and in 2012, Ann Caracristi was inducted into the National Security Agency/Central Security Service Cryptologic Hall of Honor.

In a lengthy interview for the Veterans History Project, Caracristi discussed her unusual background for a career in cryptology. In response to a question, Caracristi said that the Signal Intelligence Service contacted Women's Colleges seeking people to work on cryptography. Majors were not specified. Caracristi had very little math in her background, so she learned as she went. The people with whom she worked were mainly women; they worked hard and knew that they were contributing to the war effort. Although they were eager to be the first to solve a particular problem, the atmosphere was one of cooperation. She said, "none of us had an attitude of having to succeed or outdo another, except in trivial ways . . ."[55]

Jack Ingram, Curator of the National Cryptologic Museum relayed an anecdote in which a former NSA senior analyst was asked what cryptoanalyst he would want if he was stranded on a desert island in the Pacific and a single unbroken message could get him home. He responded "Ann Caracristi would be the one to break that message for me."[56]

---

[53] Ibid.

[54] Ibid.

[55] The Library of Congress-American Folklore Center, "Ann Caracristi Collection: Veterans History Project," accessed October 1, 2014, http://www.lcweb2.loc.gov/diglib/vhp/bib/30844.

[56] Honorary Degree Collection, Archives, The Sage Colleges.

RSC/TSC Honorary Degree Recipients

Year	Name	Degree
1929	Eliza Kellas	L.L.D.
	Anna Eleanor Roosevelt	L.D.H.
1930	Amy Morris Homans	Pd.D.
	Eva Le Gallienne	Litt.D.
	Florence Gibb Pratt	L.H.D.
1931	Ruth Bryan Owen	L.H.D.
	Lillian Moller Gilbreth	Sc.D.
1932	Katherine Kellas	Ed.D.
	Louise Homer	Mus.D.
	Mabel Smith Douglass	L.L.D.
1933	Edna St. Vincent Millay	Litt.D.
	Margaret Shove Morriss	L.L.D.
1934	Edythe Wynne Matthison	Litt.D.
	Constance Leigh	Ed.D.
	Constance Warren	Ed.D.
	Rollin C. Reynolds	L.H.M.
1935	Anne Morgan	L.H.D.
	May Peabody	Pd.D.
	Henry Thomas Moore	L.L.D.
1936	Annie Warburton Goodrich	L.L.D.
	Marie Mattingly Meloney	L.H.D.
	Fannie French Morse	Pd.D.
1937	Mary Lewis	L.H.D.
	Winifred Goldring	Sc.D.
	Josephine Bicknell Neal	Sc.D.
	Dorothy Thompson	Litt.D.
1938	Florence Sabin	Sc.D.
	Sarah Wambaugh	L.L.D.
	Nadia Boulanger	Mus.D.
1939	Irene Langhorne Gibson	L.H.D.
	Niels Bukh	Pd.D.
	Constance Amberg Sporborg	L.H.D.
	Sarah Sturtevant	Pd.D.
	Edgar Hayes Betts	L.H.D.
1940	Gertrude Angell	Ph.D.
	Frieda Miller	L.H.D.
	Gertrude Vanderbilt Whitney	L.H.D.
	Nellie Neilson	Litt.D.
	Count Rene Doynel de Saint-Quentin	L.L.D.
1941	Sigrid Undset	Litt.D.
	Emma Perry Carr	Sc.D.
	Eve Curie	L.H.D.

25TH ANNIVERSARY

Year	Name	Degree
	Ana Rosa de Martínez Guerrero	L.L.D.
	Marina Núñez del Prado	L.H.D.
	Maria Josephina R. Albano	L.H.D.
	Graciela Mandujano	L.H.D.
	Ester Niera de Calvo	Pd.D.
	Concha Romero James	L.H.D.
1942	Agnes Rebecca Wayman	Pd.D.

Year	Name	Degree
	Doris Loraine Crockett	Pd.D.
	Kathryn McHale	L.H.D.
1943	Anna Lederer Rosenberg	L.H.M.
	Marion Syddum Van Liew	Pd.D.
	Mei-ling Soong Chiang	L.L.D.
1944	Katharine Burr Blodgett	Sc.D.
	Sophie van Senden Theis	L.H.D.
	Margaret Webster	Litt.D.
1945	Mary Barnett Gilson	L.L.D.
	Mabel Newcomer	L.H.D.
	Dorothy Constance Stratton	L.H.D.
1946	Sarah Gibson Blanding	L.L.D.
	Alice Curtis Desmond	Litt.D.
	Katharine Elizabeth McBride	L.L.D.
	Lila Acheson Wallace	Litt.D.
1947	Florence Ellinwood Allen	L.L.D.
	Ruth Fulton Benedict	Sc.D.
	Emily Hickman	L.H.D.
	Alice Morgan Wright	L.H.D.
1948	Catherine Drinker Bowen	Litt.D.
	Lucy Ella Fay	Litt.D.
	Katharine Fredrica Lenroot	L.H.D.
	Agnes Ernst Meyer	L.H.D.
	Helen McKinstry	L.H.D.
1949	Maude Miner Hadden	L.H.D.
	Anna Mary Robertson Moses	L.H.D.
1950	Georgia Neese Clark	L.H.D.
	Lynn Fontanne	Litt.D.
	Dorothy Fosdick	L.L.D.
1951	Dorothy Shaver	L.H.D.
	Minnie Shafer Guggenheimer	L.H.D.
1952	Elizabeth Gray Vining	L.H.D.
1953	Agnes George de Mille	Litt.D.
	Winifred Leo Haag	L.H.D.
1954	Mary Pillsbury Lord	L.H.D.
	Doris Emrick Lee	Litt.D.
1955	Jacqueline Cochran	L.H.D.
	Leona Baumgartner	Sc.D.
1956	Margaret Chase Smith	Ll.D.
	Blanche Pittman	L.H.D.
1957	Doris Fleeson	L.H.D.
1958	Marguerite Stitt Church	Ll.D.
	Sanford Lockwood Cluett	Sc.D.
1959	May Sarton	Litt.D.
	Alma Lutz	Litt.D.
1960	Maria Goeppert Mayer	Sc.D.
	Rise Stevens	Mus.D.
1961	Ruth M. Adams	Litt.D.
	Elisabeth Achelis	L.H.D.
1962	Ester Raushenbush	Litt.D.
	Marietta Tree	L.H.D.
1963	Pauline Frederick	L.H.D.

1964	Gwendolen M. Carter	L.H.D.
	Sylvia Porter Collins	L.H.D.
	John H.G. Pell	L.H.D.
1965	Santha Rama Rau	L.H.D.
	Edna F. Kelly	L.H.D.
1966	Juanita Kidd Stout	L.H.D.
	Alice Winchester	L.H.D.

50TH ANNIVERSARY

	Millicent Mcintosh	L.H.D.
	Nancy G. Roman	Sc.D.
1967	Aline Saarinen	Litt.D.
	Edith Grace Craig Reynolds	L.H.D.
1968	Margery Somers Foster	Litt.D.
	Mildred Custin	L.H.D.
1969	Mary Elizabeth Switzer	L.H.D.
	Grace I. van Dervoort	Sc.D.
1970	Virginia Harrington Knauer	L.H.D.
	Patricia Roberts Harris	LL.D.
	Nadine Nichols Froman	L.H.D.
	Lewis Acrelius Froman	L.H.D.
1971	Chien-Shiung Wu	Sc.D.
	Elmer Schacht	L.H.D.
1972	Marina von Neumann Whitman	L.H.D.
	Dorothy L. Brown	Sc.D.
	Stephen H. Sampson	L.H.D.
1973	Virginia Apgar	L.H.D.
	Mary Anne Krupsak	L.H.D.
	Jayne Baker Spain	L.H.D.
1974	Joan Ganz Cooney	L.H.D.
	Effie O. Ellis	L.H.D.
1975	Tenley E. Albright	Sc.D.
	Catherine Blanchard Cleary	L.H.D.
	Alice Walker	Litt.D.
1976	Dixy Lee Ray	Sc.D.
	Marion S. Kellogg	Sc.D.
	Maureen Stapleton	L.H.D.
1977	Eleanor Emmons Maccoby	Sc.D.
	Donna E. Shalala	L.H.D.
	Ellen Stewart	L.H.D.
1978	Marian Wright Edelman	L.H.D.
	Carl Grimm	C.L.D
	Eve Rabin Queler	L.H.D.
1979	Esther Eggertsen Peterson	L.H.D.
	Jessie M. Scott	L.L.D.
	Charles Williams Upton	L.H.D.
	Helen Merritt Upton	L.H.D.
1980	Doris Grumbach	L.H.D.
	William Kennedy	L.H.D.
	Elizabeth Neufeld	Sc.D.
	Patricia Scott Schroeder	L.L.D.
1981	Jessie Bernard	L.H.D.
	Elizabeth Janeway	L.H.D.
	Virginia Radley	L.H.D.
1982	Claiborne Pell	L.H.D.
	Delta Emma Uphoff	Sc.D.

	Shirley Young	L.H.D.
1983	Mary Ellen Avery	Sc.D.
	Grace Murray Hopper	Sc.D.
1984	Harry Apkarian	Sc.D.
	Anna Jane Harrison	Sc.D.
1985	Carolyn Forché	Litt.D.
	Virginia Lee Harvey	L.H.D.
	Peter R. Kermani	L.H.D.
1986	Helen M. Caldicott	L.H.D.
	Cathy Guisewite	Litt.D.

70TH ANNIVERSARY CONVOCATION

	Carroll L. Estes	L.H.D.
	F. William Harder	L.H.D.
1987	Thomas Berry Brazelton	Sc.D.
	Carolyn Gold Heilbrun	L.H.D.

OPENING CONVOCATION

	Elizabeth Platt Coming	L.H.D.
	Trenna Ruston Wicks	Sc.D.
1988	Patricia Amanda Andrews	Sc.D.
	Francis Terry McNamara	D.C.
1990	Gertrude B. Elion	Sc.D.
	Robert J. Lurtsema	Mus.D.
	William Manchester	L.H.D.
	Eleanor Holmes Norton	D.P.S.
1991	Judith Blegen	D.Mus
	Phyllis Prescott Van Vleet	D.P.S.
1992	Ann Caracristi	D.P.S.
	Judy Chicago	L.H.D.
	Madeleine May Kunin	D.P.S.
1993	Colonel Nancy M. Hopfenspirger	D.P.S
	William F. Kahl	L.H.D
	Roland W. Schmitt	D.H.L
	Richard Selzer	L.H.D
1994	Marjorie Rankin	Ed.D.
	Helen Thomas	D.P.S.
1995	Madelyn Pulver Jennings	D.P.S.
	Ruth B. Purtilo	Sc.D.
1996	Carolynn Reid-Wallace	D.P.S.

80TH ANNIVERSARY

	Faith Ringgold	D.F.A.
1997	Morris Silverman	D.P.S.
	Loretta Long	D.P.S.

FOUNDERS CONVOCATION

	Constance Baker Motley	D.P.S.
1998	Blanche Wiesen Cook	D.H.L.
	Fredericka Voorhaar Slingerland	D.P.A.
1999	Ruth Ida (Jacobeth) Abram	D.P.S.
	Chris Moseley	D.H.L.
2000	Edith G. McCrea	D.A.L.
	Helen R. Connors	D.P.S
	Michael G. Dolence	Ed.D.

128

FOUNDERS CONVOCATION

	Dr. Antonia Coello Novello	D.P.S.
2001	Dr. Wallace Altes	D.P.S.
	Judith A. Ramaley	Ed.D.
	Lorraine Walker Bardsley	Ed.D.
2002	Leonard F. Tantillo	D.A.L.
	Patricia Di Benedetto Snyder	D.P.S.
	Mark 0'Connor	Ed.D.
2003	Jay Murnane	Ed.D.
	Mary Theresa Streck	Ed.D.
	William G. (Jerry) Berberet	Ed.D.
2004	Neil Golub	D.P.S.
	Lewis Golub	D.P.S.
	Anita Lucia Roddick, DBE	D.P.S.
2005	Prudence Bushnell	D.P.S.
2006	Lorraine Flaherty	D.P.S.
	Alan Chartock	D.P.S.
2007	David L. Warren	D.P.S.
2008	(None given)	
2009	Byllye Y. Avery	D.P.S.
	John Prendergast	D.P.S.
2010	William Schulz	D.Min.
	Benita Zahn	D.P.S.
2011	LouAnne Johnson	D.P.S.
	Susan Reverby	D.H.L.
2012	Anna Quindlen	D.H.L.
	HRH Princess Maha Chakri Sirindhom	D.P.S.
2013	Zoe Caldwell	D.A.L.
	Hamdi Ulukaya	D.H.L.
2014	John Bennett	D.H.L.
	Chester J. Opalka	D.H.L.
2015	Madeline Ruether Kennedy	D.P.S.
	David Allan Miller	D.H.L.
	Nancy S. Mueller	D.A.L

Selected Bibliography and Resources

Archives and Special Collections

Archives and Special Collections. Emma Willard School, Troy, New York.

Archives and Special Collections. The Sage Colleges, Troy, New York.

Books

Adams, Jean and Margaret Kimball. *Heroines of the Sky.* Garden City: Doubleday, 1942.

Allen, Florence Ellinwood. *The Constitution of Ours.* New York: G.P. Putnam's Sons, 1940.

—. *To Do Justly.* Cleveland: The Press of Western Reserve University, 1965.

Brittin, Norman A. *Edna St. Vincent Millay, Revs. Ed.* Boston: Twayne, 1982.

Brokaw, Tom. *The Greatest Generation.* New York: Random House, 1998.

Cochran, Jacqueline and Maryann Bucknum Brinley. *Jackie Cochran: An Autobiography.* New York: Bantam Books, 1987.

—and Floyd Odlum. *The Stars at Noon.* Boston: Little, Brown, 1954.

Condon, Robert J. *Great Women Athletes of the 20th Century.* Jefferson, North Carolina: McFarland & Company, Inc., 1991.

Cook, Blanche Wiesen. *Eleanor Roosevelt Volume I 1884-1933.* New York: Viking, 1992.

—. *Eleanor Roosevelt Volume II 1933-1938.* New York: Viking, 1999.

Curie, Eve. *Madame Curie.* Paris: Gallimard, 1938.

del Prado, Marina Núñez. *Eternidad en los Andes Memorias de Marina Núñez del Prado.* Editorial Lord Cochrane, 1973.

DesJardins, Julie. *The Madame Curie Complex.* New York: The Feminist Press, 2010.

DiDomenico, Kelly. *Women Scientists Who Changed the World.* New York: The Rosen Publishing Group, 2012.

Emling, Shelley. *Madame Curie and Her Daughters: The Private Lives of Science's First Family.* New York: Palgrave Macmillan, 2012.

Ferry, Joseph. *Maria Goeppert Mayer.* Philadelphia: Chelsea House 2003.

Friedman, B.H. *Gertrude Vanderbilt Whitney.* Garden City: Doubleday, 1978.

Gabor, Ándrea. *Einstein's Wife*. New York: Viking, 1995.

Gilbreth, Jr., Frank B. and Ernestine Gilbreth Carey. *Belles on Their Toes*. New York: Thomas Y. Crowell Company, 1950.

Goldring, Winifred. *Handbook of Paleontology for Beginners and Amateurs. Part 1: The Fossils*. Albany: The University of the State of New York, 1929.

— *Handbook of Paleontology for Beginners and Amateurs. Part 2: The Formations*. Albany: The University of the State of New York, 1931.

— *The Devonian Crinoids of the State of New York*. New York State Memoirs, No. 16, 1923.

Goldring, M.A., Winifred. *Guide to the Geology of John Boyd Thacher Park and Vicinity*. NY State Museum Handbook 14. Albany: The University of the State of New York, 1933.

Goodrich, Annie Warburton. *The Social and Ethical Significance of Nursing- A Series of Addresses*. New York: Macmillan, 1932.

Gosalvez, Raul Botelho and Gabriela Mistral. *Escultura de Marina Núñez del Prado*. Ediciones Galería Bonino, 1961.

Gustafson, Alrik. *Six Scandinavian Novelists*. Princeton:Princeton University Press 1940.

Hoff-Wilson, Joan and Marjorie Lightman, eds. *Without Precedent: Eleanor Roosevelt*. Bloomington: Indiana University Press, 1984.

Koch, Harriet Berger. *Militant Angel*. New York: MacMillan, 1951.

Larsen, Hanna Astrup. *Sigrid Undset*. The American-Scandinavian Review: June and July 1929, pp 2-20.

Lee, Doris. *Doris Lee*. New York: American Artists Group, 1946.

— *Images of Delight 1930-1950*. New York: D. Wigmore Fine Art, 1996.

—*A Celebration of Life 1940-1950*. New York: D.Wigmore Fine Art, 1998.

Macdougall, Allan Ross, ed. *Letters of Edna St. Vincent Millay*. New York: Grosset & Dunlap, 1952.

Mayer, Peter C. *Son of (Entropy)²*. Bloomington: Author House, 2011.

McGrayne, Sharon Bertsch. *Nobel Prize Women in Science: Their Lives, Struggles, and Momentous Discoveries*. New York: Carol Publishing, 1993.

Milford, Nancy. *Savage Beauty: the life of Edna St. Vincent Millay*. New York: Random House, 2001.

Newland, D.H., ed. *The Paleozoic Stratigraphy of New York.* Washington: United States Printing Office, 1932.

Nichols, Nikki, *Frozen in Time: The Enduring Legacy of the 1961 U.S. Figure Skating Team.* Cincinnati: Emmis Books, 2006.

Nolen, Barbara, ed. *Mexico Is People Land of Three Cultures.* New York: Charles Scribner's Sons, 1973.

Palmer, Ph.D., Norman D., ed. *The National Interest—Alone or with Others?* Philadelphia: The American Academy of Political and Social Science, 1952.

Park, Marlene and Gerald Markowitz. *Democratic vistas: post offices and public art in the New Deal.* Philadelphia: Temple University Press, 1984.

Patton, Julia. *Russell Sage College The First Twenty-Five Years 1916-1941.* Troy: Press of Walter Snyder, 1941.

Potwine, Elizabeth B. *Faithfully Yours, Eliza Kellas.* Troy: Emma Willard School, 1960.

Rock, David, ed. *Latin America in the 1940s—War and Postwar Transitions,* Berkley: University of California Press, 1994.

Roosevelt, Eleanor. *On My Own.* New York: Harper & Brothers, 1958.

Salokar, Rebecca Mae and Mary L. Volcansek, eds. *Women in Law.* Westport, CT: Greenwood Press, 1966.

Spears, George. *Russell Sage College The Second Quarter Century 1941-1966.* Troy: Birkmayer 1966.

Stratton, Dorothy C. and Helen B. Schleman. *Your Best Foot Forward,* New York: McGraw-Hill, 1955.

Tuve, Jeanette E. *First Lady of the Law.* Lanham, MD: University Press of America, 1984.

Vining, Elizabeth Gray. *Windows for the Crown Prince.* New York: J. P. Lippincott, 1952.

—*The Virginia Exiles.* New York: J.B. Lippincott, 1955.

— *Quiet Pilgrimage.* New York: J.B. Lippincott, 1970.

— *Being Seventy.* New York: The Viking Press, 1978.

Warren, Wini. *Black Women Scientists in the United States.* Bloomington: Indiana University Press, 1999.

Werminghaus, M.N. Esther A. *Annie W. Goodrich- Her Journey to Yale.* New York: Macmillan,1950.

Journals

de Martínez Guerrero, Ana Rosa. "Argentines Organize to Defend Democracy." *The Inter-American Quarterly* 3 (1941): 61-67.

Ginsburg, Ruth Bader. "Women's Progress at the Bar and on the Bench: Pathmarks In Alabama and Elsewhere in the Nation." *University of Toledo Law Review* 36 (2005): 851-53.

— and Laura W. Brill. "Address: Women in the Federal Judiciary: Three Way Pavers and the Exhilarating Change President Carter Wrought." *Fordham Law Review* 64(1995): 1-9.

Goldring, W. "Algal barrier reef in the lower Ozarkian of New York." *New York State Museum Bulletin* 315 (1938): 5-75.

Mandujano, Graciela. Program for Rural Chile." *Journal of Marriage and Family* 4 (1942): 533-35.

—. "The Education of Women in South America." *The Journal of the Association of Collegiate Alumnae* 10 (1916): 233-243.

Mayer, Joseph E. "The Way it Was." *Annual Review of Physical Chemistry* 33, no 1 (1982): 1-23.

Pernet, Corinne. "Chilean Feminists." *Woman Suffrage: The View from the Pacific* 69 (2000): 663-688. Accessed September 15, 2015. http://www.jstor.org/stable/3641229.

Pfeffer, Paula F. "Eleanor Roosevelt and the National and World Woman's Parties." *The Historian* (1996): 39-57. http://www.harvey.binghamton.edu.

Rossiter, Margaret W. "The Matilda Effect in Science." *Social Studies of Science* 23 (1993): 325-41.

Schaefer, V. J. and George L. Gaines, Jr. "Obituary: Katharine Burr Blodgett 1898-1979." *Journal of Colloid and Interface Science* 76 (1980): 269.

Suits, C. G. "Seventy-five years of Research in General Electric." *Science* 118 (1953): 451-456.

Newspapers

The Daily Boston Globe

"Highlights in Career of Ruth Bryan Owen." *Daily Boston Globe,* July 8, 1936. *ProQuest Historical Newspapers: Boston Globe (1872-1982)* (815090803).

"J. L. Meader Named Russell Sage Head." *Daily Boston Globe,* February 21, 1928. *ProQuest Historical Newspapers: Boston Globe (1872-1982)* (747567569).

"Mrs. Owen to Wed This Week: Minister to Denmark will Marry Dane She is Silent on Question of Resigning Post." *Daily Boston Globe,* July 8, 1936. *ProQuest Historical Newspapers: Boston Globe (1872-1982)* (815091380).

"Ruth Bryan Leavitt to Marry Again: Daughter of Democratic Candidate Won by Lieut R. A. Owen, R.E." *Daily Boston Globe,* April 28, 1910. *ProQuest Historical Newspapers: Boston Globe (1872-1982).* (501454533).

"Ruth Bryan Rohde, United States' First Woman Envoy, Dies." *Daily Boston Globe,* July 27, 1954. *ProQuest Historical Newspapers: Boston Globe (1872-1982)* (840073540).

"The Secret Diary of Harold L. Ickes." *Daily Boston Globe,* January 17, 1954. *ProQuest Historical Newspapers: Boston Globe (1872-1982)* (822297076).

"Women Without A Country" *Daily Boston Globe,* November 30, 1928. *ProQuest Historical Newspapers: Boston Globe (1872-1982)* (747499938).

The Hartford Courant

"Conn. Students Aid Chest Drive At Russell Sage." *The Hartford Courant,* November 19, 1939. *ProQuest Historical Newspapers: Hartford Courant (1754-1988)* (559245839).

"Dr. James L. Meader To Give Weekly Radio Talks on Education." *The Hartford Courant,* May 28, 1929. *ProQuest Historical Newspapers: Hartford Courant (1754-1988)* (557662371).

"Former State Educator New Information Chief." *The Hartford Courant,* July 13,1956. *ProQuest Historical Newspapers: Hartford Courant (1754-1988)* (563806842).

"J. L. Meader to Wed Mrs. Eleanor Virden." *The Hartford Courant,* June 8, 1946. *ProQuest Historical Newspapers: Hartford Courant (1754-1988)* (560536205).

"James L. Meader, At 35, Installed As Head of Russell Sage College." *The Hartford Courant,* February 23, 1929. *ProQuest Historical Newspapers: Hartford Courant (1754-1988)* (557627989).

"Name Meader Russell Sage College Head: Principal of New Haven Normal School and State Supervisor of Schools Chosen for Troy Post." *The Hartford Courant,* February 28, 1928. *ProQuest Historical Newspapers: Hartford Courant (1754-1988)* (557472475).

"Ruth Owen Pleads Case on Election: Bryan's Daughter Appears Before Committee in Contest Over Florida Seat in House." *The Hartford Courant,* January 19,1930. *ProQuest Historical Newspapers: Hartford Courant (1754-1988)* (557791285).

The New York Times

Altman, Lawrence K. "Gertrude Elion, Drug Developer, Dies at 81." *New York Times,* February 23, 1999. *ProQuest Historical Newspapers: The New York Times (1851-2010) with Index (1851-1993)* (110012882).

"Award at Russell Sage: Five Seniors on Cum Laude List New 'College Honors' Announced." *New York Times,* May 23, 1937. *ProQuest Historical Newspapers: The New York Times (1851-2010) with Index (1851-1993)* (102208960).

"Civic Affairs Aid Urged on Nurses: Dr. L. Meader in Convention Talk Appeals for Leadership in Community Work PROPOSES WIDER TRAINING State Group at Lake Placid Discusses Proposals for Licensing All Public Practitioners." *New York Times,* September 30, 1937. *ProQuest Historical Newspapers: The New York Times (1851-2010) with Index (1851-1993)* (102126858).

Clark, Alfred E. "Dr. Katharine Burr Blodgett, 81, Developer of Nonreflecting Glass *New York Times,* October 13, 1979. *ProQuest Historical Newspapers: The New York Times (1851-2010) with Index (1851-1993)* (123970881).

"Declares College Must Pick Student: Dr. Meader Tells Women Deans at Troy Convention That Home Has Obligations. COORDINATION IS ASKED Adjustment to Secondary School Program Is Recommended in Committee's Report. Needs Clear-Cut Objectives. Hears Coordination Report. Discusses Personal Equation. *New York Times,* November 16, 1929. *ProQuest Historical Newspapers: The New York Times (1851-2010) with Index (1851-1993)* (104831284).

"Dr. Meader Joins Army Staff." *New York Times,* March 24, 1942. *ProQuest Historical Newspapers: The New York Times (1851-2010) with Index (1851-1993)* (106300305).

"Eve D. Curie Bride of H. R. Labouisse." *New York Times,* November 20, 1954. *ProQuest Historical Newspapers: The New York Times (1851-2010) with Index (1851-1993)* (113073592).

"Florence Allen, 82, First Woman on U.S. Appellate Bench, Dead." *New York Times,* September 14, 1966. *ProQuest Historical Newspapers: The New York Times (1851-2010) with Index (1851-1993)* (1169586240).

"Heads Gimbels Division of Customer Relations." *New York Times,* May 21, 1947. *ProQuest Historical Newspapers: The New York Times (1851-2010) with Index (1851-1993)* (107931256).

Hechinger, Fred M. "About Education: When motherhood interferes with the Training of young female scientists." *New York Times,* November 9, 1988. *ProQuest Historical Newspapers: The New York Times (1851-2010) with Index (1851-1993)* (110435219).

"Major Reginald Owen: Son-in-Law of Bryan Succumbs to Illness Contracted in War." *New York Times*, December 13, 1927. *ProQuest Historical Newspapers: The New York Times (1851-2010) with Index (1851-1993)* (104056977).

Markoff, John. "Rear Adm. Grace M. Hopper Dies; Innovator in Computers Was 85." *New York Times,* January 3, 1992. *ProQuest Historical Newspapers: The New York Times (1851-2010) with Index (1851-1993)* (108870651).

Meader, James L. "Futility of War" *New York Times,* November 11, 1934. *ProQuest Historical Newspapers: The New York Times (1851-2010) with Index (1851-1993)* (101202102).

— "Will Stress Amity With Latin America." *New York Times,* August 31, 1941. *ProQuest Historical Newspapers: The New York Times (1851-2010) with Index (1851-1993)* (105982780).

Millay, Edna St. Vincent. " 'There Are No Islands, Any More': Lines Written in Passion And in Deep Concern for England, France and My Own Country." *New York Times,* June 14, 1940. *ProQuest Historical Newspapers: The New York Times (1851-2010) with Index (1851-1993)* (105412946).

"Miss Eliza Kellas, Educator, is Dead." *New York Times*, April 11, 1943. *ProQuest Historical Newspapers: The New York Times (1851-2010) with Index (1851-1993)* (106711834).

"Mrs. Ana de Martinez Guerro of Argentina, Foe of Peron, Dies." *New York Times,* September 05, 1964. *ProQuest Historical Newspapers: The New York Times (1851-2010) with Index (1851-1993)* (115624974).

"Mrs. Owens Defends Her Citizenship." *New York Times*, January 19, 1930. *ProQuest Historical Newspapers: The New York Times (1851-2010) with Index (1851-1993)* (99024915).

"Neutrality Debate Set at Russell Sage: Students Called On to Study America's Responsibility." *New York Times,* October 1, 1939. *ProQuest Historical Newspapers: The New York Times (1851-2010) with Index (1851-1993)* (103077533).

"Refuses Support for Another War." *New York Times,* November 7, 1934. *ProQuest Historical Newspapers: The New York Times (1851-2010) with Index (1851-1993)* (101226284).

"Russell Sage College to Aid Idle." *New York Times*, June 2, 1933. *ProQuest Historical Newspapers: The New York Times (1851-2010) with Index (1851-1993)* (100670570).

"Russell Sage Gets a Spanish House" *New York Times,* October 15, 1939. *ProQuest Historical Newspapers: The New York Times (1851-2010) with Index (1851-1993)* (103089431).

"Russell Sage Links College and 'Career' By Combining Cultural and Nurse Training" *New York Times*, January 16, 1938. *ProQuest Historical Newspapers: The New York Times (1851-2010) with Index (1851-1993)* (102686496).

"Russell Sage Plans 4-Year Nursing Study: Degree Course is Mapped to Provide Professional Basis – Albany Hospital to Aid." *New York Times,* May 5, 1934. *ProQuest Historical Newspapers: The New York Times (1851-2010) with Index (1851-1993)* (101576250).

"Russell Sage Spurs Liberal Arts Studies: Courses Are Being Rearranged for Next Semester to Emphasize the Courses." *New York Times*, December 5, 1937. *ProQuest Historical Newspapers: The New York Times (1851-2010) with Index (1851-1993)* (102170690).

"Ruth Bryan Owen Envoy to Denmark." *New York Times,* April 13, 1933. *ProQuest Historical Newspapers: The New York Times (1851-2010) with Index (1851-1993)* (100729371).

"Russell Sage Widens Faculty Influence: Council to Have Decisive Voice in Educational Policies." *New York Times,* December 11, 1938. *ProQuest Historical Newspapers: The New York Times (1851-2010) with Index (1851-1993)* (102492326).

Saxon, Wolfgang. "Georgia Neese Clark Gray, 95, First Woman as U.S. Treasurer." *New York Times Late Edition East Coast*, October 28, 1995. *ProQuest Historical Newspapers: The New York Times with Index* (430333344).

Smith, Roberta. "Offering a Painter for History's Reconsideration." *New York Times,* April 7, 2008. *ProQuest Historical Newspapers: The New York Times with Index* (897133548).

"Tells Who Belongs At Russell Sage: Dr. Meader Puts Thinking and Living Before Scholarship in College Education." *New York Times*, November 6, 1938. *ProQuest Historical Newspapers: The New York Times (1851-2010) with Index (1851-1993)* (102411057).

"The Leavitt-Bryan Wedding: Preparations Under Way to Make It an Elaborate Society Event." *New York Times,* September 23, 1903. *ProQuest Historical Newspapers: The New York Times (1851-2010) with Index (1851-1993)* (96327736).

"Will Head Russell Sage: Dr. Meader Goes to College at Troy-Deanship Is Also Changed." *New York Times,* February 21, 1928. *ProQuest Historical Newspapers: The New York Times (1851-2010) with Index (1851-1993)* (104641381).

The Times

"Eve Curie." *The Times,* October 26, 2007. *ProQuest Newstand* (319801355).

Times-Union

Arnold, Jeanne. "Her Dream Came True." *Times-Union*, May 21, 1972, B-4.

Videodiscs

Burns, Ken, Geoffrey C. Ward, Paul Barnes, Pam Tubridy Baucom, Peter Coyote, Paul Giamatti, Edward Hermann, et al. 2014. *The Roosevelts: an intimate history.*

Websites

AAUW. "Meet Marina Núñez del Prado." Accessed August 13, 2015. http://www.aauw.org/2012/02/22/meet-marina-nunez-del-prado-famed- bolivian-artist/

About.com. "Lillian Moller Gilbreth (1878-1972)." Accessed September 30, 2014. http://www.inventors.about.com/library/inventors/blgilbreth.htm.

Academy of Achievement. "Tenley Albright-Interview." Accessed August 18, 2015. http://www.achievement.org/autodoc/page/albOint-1.

African American Registry. "Surgical Pioneer, Dorothy L. Brown." Accessed February 21, 2014. http://www.aaregistry.org.

Aldrich, Michele L., Alan E. Leviton, and Mark Aldrich. "Winifred Goldring (1888-1971, New York Paleontologist." Geological Society of America. Accessed February 25, 2008. http://gsa.confex.com/gsa/2005NE/finalprogram/abstract_82915.htm.

American National Biography. "Georgia Neese Clark." Rossiter. Accessed October 24, 2014. http://www.anb.org.

Archives of American Art, Smithsonian Institution. "Oral History Interview with Doris Emrick Lee, 1964 Nov. 4." Accessed November 20, 2014. http://www.aaa.si.edu/collections/interviews/oral-history-interview-doris-emrick-lee 12289#transcript.

Argonne National Laboratory. "Maria Goeppert Mayer." Accessed February 24, 2014. http://www.ne.anl.gov.

Avery, Mary Ellen. "Gertrude B. Elion January 23, 1918-February 21, 1999." National Academy of Sciences. Accessed March 17, 2008. http://www.nap.edu/html/biomems/gelion.html.

Brown, Patrick (reprocessed). "Guide to the Doris Lee Papers 1924-1987." Archives And Special Collections National Museum of Women in the Arts. Accessed November 20, 2014. http://www.nmwa.org.

Busca Biografías. "Esther Neira de Calvo." Accessed September 15, 2015. http://www.buscabiografias.com/biografia/verDetalle/9634/Esther Neira de Calvo.

Casa. Museo Núñez del Prado. "Marina Núñez del Prado" Accessed August 13, 2015. www.bolivian.com/cmplinindex.html.

California State University, Pomona. "Lillian Moller Gilbreth." Accessed February 3, 2014. http://www.csupomona.edu/~plin/inventors/gilbreth.html.

Coast Guard News. "First Lady Christens Coast Guard Cutter Dorothy C. Stratton." Accessed March 3, 2014. http://www.coastguardnews.com.

Columbia-Presbyterian Medical Center. "Virginia Apgar: A Legend Becomes a Postage Stamp." Accessed August 15, 2015. http://www.cumc.columbia.edu/psjournal/archives.

Conselho Regional de Servico Social. "Maria Josephina Rabello Albano – The Challenging Intrepid. Accessed September 15, 2015. http://www.cressrj.org.br/download/arquivos/artigo-Maria-josephina-2012-.pdf.

Congressional Biographical Directory. "Ruth Bryan Owen (1885-1954)." Accessed February 18 2008, http://www.bioguide.congress.gov/scripts/.

Dickason, Elizabeth. "Grace Mary Hopper." about.com. Accessed November 20, 2014, http://www.inventors.about.com.

Elion, Gertrude B. "Autobiography." Nobel Prize Organization. Accessed March 17, 2008, http://www.nobelprize.org.

Embassy of the United States Copenhagen, Denmark. "Ruth Bryan Owen." Accessed March 3, 2014. http://www.Denmark.usembassy.gov/about-us/history/rbo.html.

Encyclopedia.com. "Tenley Emma Albright." Accessed September 18, 2015. http://www.encyclopedia.com/topic/Tenley_Emma_Albright.aspx.

— "Mayer, Maria Goeppert." Accessed February 24, 2014. http://www.encyclopedia.com/topicMaria_Goeppert_Mayer.aspx.

Encylopedia Britannica. "Gertrude Vanderbilt Whitney," accessed March 3, 2008, http://www.britannica.com.

Fee-Thomson, Robbie, "Capt. Dorothy Stratton Remembered: Her Life and Legacy." Accessed October 23, 2014. http://www.womensmemorial.org.

First Ladies Organization. "First Lady Biography: Eleanor Roosevelt." Accessed March 3, 2014. http://www.firstladies.org.

Firstenberg, Nora. "Marriage and Mortality: Examining the International Marriage Broker Regulation Act- A. History of Marriage and U.S. Citizenship." Accessed October 22, 2014. http://www.racism.org.

Georgetown University. "Biographical Notes." Accessed September 15, 2015. https://repository.library.georgetown.edu/bitstream/handle/10822/558706/GTM.071217.html?sequence=1.

Graham, Laurel D. "Lillian Gilbreth's psychologically enriched scientific management of women consumers. 2013." Academia.edu. Accessed September 30, 2014. http://www.academia.edu/4552824/Lillian_Gilbreth_psychologically_enriched_scientific_mangement_of_women_ Consumers.2013.

Great American Judges: An Encyclopedia. "Allen, Florence Ellinwood." Accessed February 10, 2014. http://www.s9.com/Biography/Print/Allen-Florence- Ellinwood.

Hill Air Force Base Library. "Jacqueline Cochran." Accessed February 19, 2014. http://www.hill.af.mil/library/factsheets.asp?id=5861.

Home.frog. "Katharine B. Blodgett." Accessed February 21, 2014. http://www.home.frog.net/-ejcov/blodgett2.html.

Kansas Historical Society. "Georgia Neese Clark Gray." Accessed October 24, 2014. http://www.kshs.org.

Lewis, Jone Johnson. "Maria Goeppert-Mayer." about.com. Accessed February 24, 2014. http://www.womenshistoryabout.com.

National Institute of Medicine. "Dr. Tenley E. Albright." Accessed September 18, 2015. http://www.nim.nih.gov/changingthefaceof medicine.

National Inventors Hall of Fame. "Katharine Burr Blodgett." Accessed February 21, 2014. http://www.invent.org/hall_of_fame/319.html.

National Library of Medicine. "Dr. Dorothy Lavinia Brown." Accessed February 2014. http://www.nlm.nih.gov.

"The Virginia Apgar Papers." Accessed February 19, 2014. http://www.profiles.nlm.nih.gov.

National Museum of Woman Artists. "Marina Núñez del Prado." Accessed August 13, 2015. http://www.clara.nmwa.org/index.php?g=entity_detail&entity_id=6289.

National Park Service. "Judge Florence Allen Biography." Accessed September 10, 2015. http://www.nps.gov/room/judge_florence_allen_biography.htm.

National Security Agency. "Ann Caracristi: 2012 Inductee." Accessed October 1, 2014. http://www.nsa.gov.

National Womens Hall of Fame. "Florence Ellinwood Allen." Accessed February 03, 2014. http://www.greatwomwn.org/women-of–the-hall/search-the-hall-result…

Netherland Institute. "Gertrude Vanderbilt Whitney (1875-1942) Notable Dutch-American." Accessed February 3, 2014. http://www.netherlandinstitute.org.

New York State Museum. "Gilboa Devonian Forest Exhibit." Accessed February 25, 2008. http:// www.nysm.nysed.gov.

Nobel Prize Organization. "Maria Goeppert Mayer." Accessed February 21, 2014. http://www.nobelprize.org.

— "The Nobel Prize in Literature 1928." Accessed February 21, 2014. www.nobelprize. org/nobelprizes/literature/laureates/1928/undset-facts.html.

Ohio History Connection. "Florence E. Allen." Accessed September 10, 2015. http:// www.ohiohistorycentral.org/w/Florence_E._Allen.

Owen (Rohde), Ruth Bryan. "Reclaiming the Everglades." Florida International University. Accessed March 3, 2014. http://www.everglades.fiu.edu.

Purdue Libraries, Archives and Special Collections. "Dorothy C. Stratton papers, 1935-2006." Accessed March 3, 2014. http://www.4.lib.purdue/edu/.

Purdue University. "Dorothy C. Stratton, Purdue's first Dean of Women, dies at 107," Accessed November 17, 2014. http://www.purdue.edu.

Robinson, Scott. "Georgia Neese Clark Gray." Robinson Library. Accessed October 24, 2014. http://www.robinsonlibrary.com.

Roosevelt, Franklin. "Address before the Governing Board of the Pan American Union. White House, 27 May 1941." Center for the Public Domain and the University of North Carolina. Accessed August 2, 2014. http://www.ibiblio.org.

—"Third Inaugural Address, 20 January 1941." *The American Presidency Project."* Online by Gerhard Peters and John T. Wooley. Accessed August 2, 2014. http://www. presidency.uscb.edu/ws/?pid=16022.

—"Proclamation of Unlimited National Emergency, 27 May 1941." Center for the Public Domain and the University of North Carolina. Accessed August 2, 2014. http://www.ibiblio.org.

San Diego Supercomputer Center. "Maria Goeppert-Mayer." Accessed February 3, 2014. http://www.sdsc.edu/ScienceWomen/mayer.html.

State of Utah. "Florence Ellinwood Allen." Accessed September 10, 2015. http://www.historytogo.utah.gov/people/utahns_of_achievement/florenceellinwoodallen.html.

Tenley. "Tenley E. Albright MD." Accessed September 18, 2015. http://www.mynameis tenley.com/about-tenley-albright/

The Happiest Home. "Housekeeping, techology, and happiness – according to Lillian Gilbreth." Accessed September 30, 2014. http://www.thehappiesthome.com/ housekeeping-techology-and-happiness-according-to-lillian-gilbreth.

The Library of Congress-American Folklife Center. "Ann Caracristi Collection: Veterans History Project." accessed October 1, 2014. http://www.lcweb2.loc.gov/diglib/ vhp/bib/30844.

The Washington Post. "Esther de Calvo, 87, Former Envoy to OAS." Accessed September 15, 2015. http:??www.washingtonpost.com/archive/local/1978/03/26/esther-de-calvo-87-former-envoy-to OAS.

UCLA. "Katharine Burr Blodgett." Accessed February 21, 2014. http://www.cwp. library.ucla.edu.

U.S. Department of Homeland Security. "Dorothy C. Stratton." Accessed March 2, 2014. http://www.uscg.mil/history/people/DStrattonBio.asp.

U.S. House of Representatives. "Representative Ruth Bryan Owen of Florida." Accessed October 22, 2014. http://www.history.house.gov.

— "Ruth Bryan Owen." Accessed March 3, 2014. http://www.history.house.gov.

—"The swearing-in of Representatives Ruth Bryan Owen of Florida and Ruth Hanna McCormick of Illinois." Accessed October 22, 2014. http://www.history.house.gov.

University of Kansas. "Georgia Neese Gray." Accessed October 24, 2014. http://www. emilytaylorcenter.ku.edu/pioneer-Woman/gray.

Webster University. "Lillian Moller Gilbreth." Accessed September 30, 2014. http:// www2.webster.edu.

Women in World History: A Biographical Encyclopedia. "Dorothy Stratton (b.1899)." Accessed March 2, 2014. http://www.encyclopedia.com/article-1G2591308915/stratton.